HOT Springs
& Hot Pools
of the Northwest

HOT Springs
& Hot Pools
of the Northwest

Jayson Loam's Original Guide

Marjorie Gersh-Young

AQUA THERMAL ACCESS

Grateful acknowledgements:

Bruce Saltzman, Ilene Bonomo, and Jan Stiles—all of whom went beyond their job description to offer advice and suggestions. All of the regional contributors who always went above and beyond their assignment to make this book interesting and accurate. Jerry McKee for his information on the trip down the Middle Fork Salmon River. Mary Stensvold and Leslie Murray for their help on the Alaskan "naturals." Staff members at state parks, national forests, national parks, and hot springs resorts for their cooperation and encouragement. All of you who have written in with updates and information. Henry Young (my husband) for acting as my sounding board and making the computer run right.

Front Cover - Chattanooga, Idaho / Bob Seal
Back Cover - Molly's Tubs, Idaho / Bob Seal

Hot Springs and Hot Pools of the Northwest: Jayson Loams' Original Guide

Copyright 1995 by Marjorie Gersh-Young

Design, layout and production
by Marjorie Gersh-Young

ISBN 0-9624830-7-9

Manufactured in the United States

Published by: **Aqua Thermal Access**
55 Azalea Lane
Santa Cruz, CA 95060

Photo Credits

Marlene Campbell: 28T. Susan Carter: 89T, 98T, 141, 142. S. Russell Criswell: 170. Marjorie Gersh-Young: 8, 86. Justine Hill: 12, 49, 50, 51, 83L, 84, 85T, 87, 97L, 151RT, 153, 154T, 155, 156L, 165, 167, 171RTB, 174, 175. David Hummel: 154B, 173. Jayson Loam: 9, 17T, 39, 46, 55R, 57, 59, 62, 64R, 66L, 67, 68B, 69, 70L, 71L, 72, 73B, 75, 79, 80L, 83R, 88 91, 92L, 99, 104R, 105, 106L, 111, 113-125, 133R, 134-136, 137L, 139, 145, 147L, 148L, 1551L, RB, 152, 156R, 157-159, 162, 163L, 164, 166, 169, 171L. Jerry McKee: 92R, 93-96. Bob Seal: 85R, 89B, 97R, 98 RB, LB, 100, 102, 103, 104L, 106R, 107-110, 112, 128, 129, 130-132, 133L, 137R, 138, 140, 143, 144, 147R, 149, 168, 172. Rick Slobodian: 15, 36-38, 41-45 Douglas Westphall: 28B. Phil Wilcox: 14R, 16, 18L, 24, 26, 27, 32-35, 52L, 53, 54, 55L, 56, 58, 61, 62, 63L, 64, 65, 66R, 68T, 70R, 71R, 73T, 74, 76, 80R, 81, 146, 184.

Commercial establishments contributing photos

Ainsworth Hot Springs, Alaskan Hotel, Arlington Resort Hotel, Berkeley Springs State Park (Stephen J. Shalati, Jr), Breitenbush Hot Springs, Cottonwood Hot Springs, Crystal Spa, Cypress Cove Nudist Resort, Elms Resort Hotel, Ethos Trace, Evans Plunge, The Fairmount Hotel (Canada), Fountain of Youth RV Park, Granite Creek Hot Springs (WY), The Greenbrier, Holiday Inn (WY), The Homestead, Hot Springs Hilton, Hot Springs Water Park, Inn at Soap Lake, Kah-Nee-Ta Vacation Resort, Libby Memorial Hot Springs Health Spa, Lodge at Riggins Hot Springs (Andy Hedden-Nicely), Manitou Springs Mineral Spa, Riverside Inn, Safety Harbor Spa, Sand Springs Pool, Sol Duc, Sunny Chinooks (Patrick Kornak), Tolovana (Tom De Long), Wrangell Ranger District.

To

Jayson Loam
"King of the Hot Springs"
who pursued with passion
what he truly loved to do most
and, therefore, benefited us all.
May you soak in peace.

Alaska
Page 22

HOT Springs
& Hot Pools
of the Northwest

CANADA
Page 30

British
Columbia

Alberta

**States East of
the Rockies
Page 176**

AQUA THERMAL ACCESS

Washington
Page 48

Montana
Page 150

Oregon
Page 60

Idaho
Page 82

Wyoming
Page 160

Companion volume to
Hot Springs and Hot Pools of the Southwest

TABLE OF CONTENTS

Jayson Loam
August 29, 1918 - February 22, 1994

Jayson Loam's life was a celebration of the things he loved to do, a choice earned by what he called "having paid his dues." He meant that he had put in the time, often doing things he was not all that fond of, to gain both the knowledge and the funding in order not to commit the only sin in the world that he recognized—doing anything other than what you love to do. Researching hot springs and sharing his knowledge is what he loved to do most. And, he taught me to love it too.

I have decided that the best way I can honor his life is to continue writing and publishing the hot springs books. I joyfully continue in the tradition he established so that all of you can continue to experience the best that was Jayson.

In that spirit, I have chosen to include his *Introduction,* which explains his criteria for choosing what was initially included in this book and for deciding how it was presented. I feel blessed that he had the confidence in me to want me to continue his work when he died, even though he knew that we sometimes differed as to approach and debated what was important and even what was fun. I needed more detailed directions, even with a map. I wanted more adjectives to describe what I would find when I arrived at a certain location. And I enjoyed finding out the history of a place. All of these aspects I have enlarged upon, while at the same time being careful to include the details Jayson demanded and to be as precise as possible.

I feel sure that the blending of our styles and interests will ensure you, the user, of continued enjoyment from our books.

Marjorie Gersh-Young

Introduction

by Jayson Loam

This is a book for people to use, not an academic discussion of geothermal phenomena. For me there is a special joy and contentment that comes from soaking in a sandy-bottom pool of flowing natural mineral water, accompanied by good friends and surrounded by the peaceful quiet of a remote, primitive setting. At such an idyllic moment it is hard to get overly concerned about geology, chemistry, or history. In this book it is my intent to be of service to others who also like to soak in peace and who could use some help finding just the right place.

The cataclysmic folding and faulting of the earth's crust over millions of years is a fascinating subject, especially where geologic sources have combined just the right amount of underground water with just the right amount of earth core magma to produce a hot surface flow that goes on for centuries. It would probably be fun to research and write about all that, including new data on geothermal power installations, but that is not what this book is about.

Many hot springs have long histories of special status with Indian tribes that revered the healing and peace-making powers of the magic waters. Those histories often include bloody battles with "white men" over hot spring ownership, and there are colorful legends about Indian curses that had dire effects for decades on a whole series of ill-fated owners who tried to deny Indians their traditional access to a sacred tribal spring. That, too, would be an interesting theme for a book someday, but not this book.

In the 19th century it was legal, and often quite profitable, to claim that mineral water from a famous spa had the ability to cure an impressive list of ailments. Such advertising is no longer legal, and modern medicine does not include mineral water soaks, or drinks, in its list of approved treatments. Nevertheless, quite a few people still have an intuitive feeling that, somehow, spending time soaking in natural mineral water is beneficial. I agree with the conclusion that it is "good for you," but it would take an entire book to explore all of the anecdotal and scientific material that would be needed to explain why. Someone else will have to write that book.

This book simply accepts the fact that hot springs do exist, that they have a history, and that soaking the human body in geothermal water does indeed contribute to a feeling of well-being. That still leaves several substantial, practical questions. "Where can I go to legally put my body in hot water, how do I get there, and what will I find when I arrive?" The purpose of this book is to answer those questions.

When I began to design this book, I had to decide which geothermal springs would be left out because they are not "hot." Based on my own experience, I picked 90 degrees as the cut-off point and ignored any hot springs or hot wells below that level, unless a commercial operator was using electricity, gas, or steam to bump up the temperature of the mineral water.

The second decision I had to make was whether or not to include geothermal springs on property that was fenced and posted or otherwise not accessible to the public. There are a few hot spring enthusiasts who get an extra thrill out of penetrating such fences and soaking in "forbidden" mineral water. It was my conclusion that I would be doing my readers a major disservice if I guided them into a situation where they might get arrested or shot. Therefore, I do not provide a descriptive listing for such hot springs, but I do at least mention the names of several such well-known locations in the index, with the notation NUBP, which means "Not Usable By the Public."

And then there were several more pleasant decisions, such as whether to include hot wells. Technically, they are not hot springs, but real geothermal water does flow out of them, so, if a soaking pool is accessible to the public, I chose to include it.

Within the last 30 years the radical idea of communal soaking in a redwood or fiberglass hot tub

Marjorie Gersh-Young at *Buckeye Hot Springs* (Calif.): While not always convenient for a soak, it is one of those places that I feel combines the ideal conditions of beautiful scenery, river-side pools, and plenty of hot water. Here I am taking advantage of some of the perks while doing research.

filled with gas-heated tap water has grown into a multi-million-dollar business. Thousands of residential tubs are installed every year, all of the larger motels and hotels now have at least one, and there are now dozens of urban establishments that offer private-space hot tub rentals by the hour. I chose to include rent-a-tub locations, which is why the book title is *Hot Springs and Hot Pools*.

Early on I realized that there is no such thing as a "typical" hot spring and that there is no such thing as a "typical" hot spring enthusiast. Some readers will have a whole summer vacation to trek from one remote, primitive hot spring to another. Others will be trying to make the most of a two-week vacation, a long weekend, a Saturday, or a few hours after a hard day's work. Some readers will have a self-contained RV, while others must depend on air travel and airport transportation connections. Some readers will want to find skinny-dippers, while others will want to avoid them.

Whatever your schedule, transportation, and modesty needs, this book is intended to help you make an informed choice and then get to the locations you have chosen.

Regional Contributors

Justine Hill is a travel writer/photographer/visual anthropologist who has traveled extensively and has written about and photographed other cultures, travel locations, sacred sites, and the great outdoors.

She currently lives surrounded by nature in Topanga, California, where she has a stock of over 50,000 photos that appear frequently in calendars, posters, magazines, postcards, travel literature and coffee-table books. For information about her photo collection and related services, contact Justine Hill at PO Box 608, Topanga, CA 90290. Phone: (310) 455-3409.

Phil Wilcox, also known as "the Solar Man," is semi-retired and lives on a remote piece of land in Northern California. He loves to travel often in search of hot springs, and has recently been seen in Alaska, Canada, Oregon, Washington, New Mexico and points west. When not traveling he designs, sells, and installs remote home solar power systems. Send $4.00 for a complete catalog to THE SOLAR MAN, 20560 Morgan Valley Rd., Lower Lake, CA 95457.

Bob Seal, along with his wife Glenna, his family, and his friends, do all of us hot-spring enthusiasts a favor by continually visiting, investigating, and photographing hot springs in Idaho, where he lives. He considers it the best way to spend a summer—we agree. Thanks.

Rick Slobodian was introduced to hot water at an early age when his family went on Sunday drives to Banff, where Rick (then only one year old) bathed and splashed in the many springs in the area.

Rick and Oksana met at a hot spring in 1990. Rick introduced Oksana to more hot springs, and Oksana introduced Rick to nudism. Together they have visited approximately 60 hot springs in the Pacific Northwest. It is likely their new son Austin will carry on the quest, searching, tending to, and enjoying these treasures of mother earth.

Banff Hot Springs attracted more than dignified people coming to "take the waters" in the '20s and '30s. This was new world music—jazz, and a new world way to enjoy it—at a destination resort hot spring.

HUNTING FOR HOT WATER:
A Bit of History

Long before the "white man" arrived to "discover" hot springs, the American Indians believed that the Great Spirit resided in the center of the earth and that "Big Medicine" fountains were a special gift from The Creator. Even during tribal battles over camping areas or stolen horses, it was customary for the sacred "smoking waters" to be a neutral zone where all could freely be healed of their wounds. Way back then, hot springs did indeed belong to everyone, and understandably, we would like to believe that nothing has changed.

Most of us also have a mental picture of an ideal hot spring. It will have crystal clear water, of course, with the most beneficial combination of minerals but with no slimy algae or rotten egg smells. Water temperature will be "just right" when you first step in, as well as after you have soaked for a while. It will occupy a picturesque rock-rimmed pool with a soft, sandy bottom, divided into a shallow section for lie-down soaks and a deeper section for sit-up-and-talk soaks. Naturally, it will have gorgeous natural surroundings with grass, flowers,and trees, plus an inspiring view of snow-capped mountains. The location will be so remote that you have the place to yourself and can skinny-dip if you choose, but not so remote that you might get tired from a long hike. Finally, if you like to camp out, there will be a lovely campground with rest rooms conveniently nearby or, if you prefer more service, a superior motel/restaurant just a short drive down the road.

Oh yes, this ideal spring will also be located on public land and therefore belong to everyone, just like all other hot springs. That leaves only the problem of finding that ideal spring, or, better yet, lots of them.

The "good book" for hot spring seekers is the Thermal Springs List of the United States, published by the National Oceanic and Atmospheric Administration and available through the NOAA Environmental and Data Service office in Boulder, Colorado. This publication contains nearly 1,600 entries, with nearly all of them in the 11 western states. It would be nice if all of them really existed and were easily accessible, but unfortunately, the real world of geothermal water is not quite that magical. We found that only seven percent of the listed springs are on public land, accessible without charge and another 15 percent were private, commercial enterprises open to the public.

Our hot springs research program did start with an analysis of the NOAA springs list. We noticed that nearly one-third of the locations had temperatures below 90°, so we eliminated them as simply not hot enough. The other two-thirds required individual investigation, usually involving personal inspection, result in the usable 22 percent. The unusable 88 percent were often old resorts which had burned down, seeps too small to get into or functioning as cattle troughs, or on posted, private land, making them not usable by the public (NUBP).

The Indian tradition of free access to hot springs was initially imitated by the pioneers. However, as soon as mineral water was perceived to have some commercial value, the new settler's private property laws were invoked at most of the hot spring locations. After many fierce legal battles, and a few gun battles, some ambitious settlers were able to establish clear legal titles to the properties. Then it was up to the new owners to figure out how to turn their geothermal flow into cash flow.

Pioneering settlers dismissed as superstition the Indian's spiritual explanation of the healing power of a hot spring. However, those settlers did know from experience that it was beneficial to soak their bodies in mineral water, even if they didn't know why or how

it worked. Commercial exploitation began when the owner of a private hot spring first started charging admission, ending centuries of free access.

The shift from outdoor soaks to indoor soaks began when proper Victorian customers demanded privacy, which required the erection of canvas enclosures around the bathers in the outdoor springs. Then affluent city dwellers, as they became accustomed to indoor plumbing and modern sanitation, were no longer willing to risk immersion in a muddy-edged, squishy-bottom mineral spring, even if they believed that such bathing would be good for their health. Furthermore, they learned to like their urban comforts too much to trek to an outdoor spring in all kinds of weather. Instead, they wanted a civilized method of "taking the waters," and the great spas of Europe provided just the right model for American railroad tycoons and land barons to follow, and to surpass.

Around the turn of the century, American hot spring resorts fully satisfied the combined demands of Victorian prudery, modern sanitation, and indoor comfort by offering separate men's and women's bathhouses, with private individual porcelain tubs, marble shower rooms and central heating. Scientific

At *Lolo Hot Springs* Clark wrote, "...I observe after the indians remaining in the hot bath as long as they could bear it run and plunge themselves into the creek the water of which is now as cold as ice can make it"....

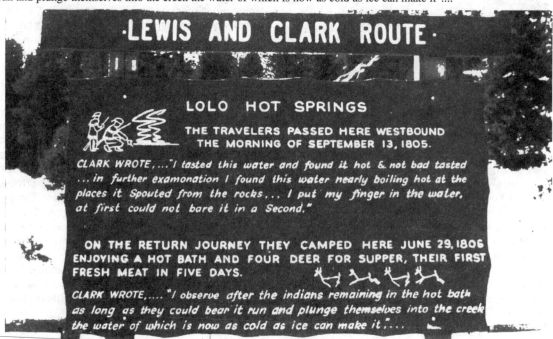

This sternwheeler used to take passengers up the lake from Nakusp to Halcyon Hot Springs. It was the only transportation to the hotel and to another hot spring, St. Leon, until Highway 23 was built in the 1950s. Neither Halcyon nor the St. Leon resort still exist, although you can still soak in the pools at Halcyon.

mineral analysis of the geothermal water was part of every resort merchandising program, which included flamboyant claims of miraculous cures and glowing testimonials from medical doctors. Their promotion material also featured additional social amenities, such as luxurious suites, sumptuous restaurants, and grand ballrooms.

In recent decades, patronage of these resorts has declined, and many have closed down because the traditional medical claims were outlawed and modern medical plans refuse to reimburse anyone for a mineral water "treatment." A few of the larger resorts have managed to survive by adding new facilities such as golf courses, conference and exhibition spaces, fitness centers, and beauty salons. The smaller hot spring establishments have responded to modern demand by installing larger (six persons or more) communal soaking tubs and family-size soaking pools in private spaces for rent by the hour. Most locations continue to offer

men's and women's bathhouse facilities in addition to the new communal pools, but most have discontinued the use of cast iron, one-person bath tubs.

In addition to the privately owned hot spring facilities, there are several dozen locations that are owned by federal, state, county, or city agencies. States, counties, and cities usually staff and operate their own geothermal installations. However, locations in the US National Forests and National Parks are usually operated under contract by privately owned companies. The nature and quality of the mineral water facilities offered at these publicly-owned, but privately operated, hot spring locations varies widely.

Although natural mineral water (from a spring or well) is required for a truly authentic traditional "therapeutic soak," there is a new generation of dedicated soakers who will not patronize a motel unless it

Hot Springs

Indians, pioneers and 1920s travellers bathed in these pools. According to legend, both the Olympic and Sol Duc Hot Springs (in Soleduck Valley) are the result of hot tears shed by two creatures who fought a frustrating battle neither could win. The tears at Olympic Hot Springs range from lukewarm to 188°F.

Sol Duc and Olympic Hot Springs are chemically similar. Ordinary surface water seeps down until it reaches the earth's hotter interior. Then, through cracks in the rock, steam and heated water rise to form the springs.

The National Park Service will maintain modern bathing facilities at Sol Duc and keep these Olympic Hot Springs in a natural state. Enjoy them, but help us preserve these "legendary tears." Please do not litter, or use plastic liners, or alter the pools in any way.

has a hot pool. They know full well that the pool is filled with gas-heated tap water, and treated with chlorine, but it is almost as good as the real thing and a lot more convenient. We chose to include in our hunt for hot water those locations that offer private-space hot tubs for rent by the hour.

According to California legend, the historic red-wood tub was invented by a Santa Barbara group who often visited Big Caliente Hot Springs. One evening a member of the group wished out loud that they could have their delicious outdoor communal soaks without having to endure the long dusty trips to and from the springs. Another member of the group suggested that a large redwood wine cask might be used as an alternate soaking pool in the city. It was worth a try, and it was a success. Over time, other refugees from the long Big Caliente drive began to build their own group soaking pools from wine casks, and the communal hot tub era was born.

Riverside Inn, Idaho, uses a new wooden tub for soaking.

Olympic Hot Springs in the state of Washington has a long and varied history dating from its first use by Native Americans, who created a legend about how the place was formed. It was also a resort that burned down many years ago. The only remnants are some foundations found near one of the springs. Until recently the road went all the way up to the springs. Now it requires a two-mile hike along the road, which is gradually being allowed to return to its natural state.

Olympic Hot Springs is one of those places where clothing-optional (some with suits, some without) really seems to work, even though the officially posted policy prohibits nudity.

A Word about Nudity

You had best start with the hard fact that any private property owner, county administration, park superintendent, or forest supervisor has the authority to prohibit "public nudity" in a specific area or in a whole park or forest. Whenever the authorities have to deal with repeated complaints about nude bathers at a specific hot spring, it is likely that the area will be posted with NO NUDITY ALLOWED signs, and you could get a citation without further warning.

The vast majority of natural hot springs on public property are not individually posted, but most jurisdictions have some form of general regulation prohibiting public nudity. However, there have been some recent court cases establishing that a person could not be found guilty of indecent exposure if he removed his clothes only after traveling to a remote area where there was no one to be offended.

In light of these court cases, one of the largest national forests has retained its general "nude bathing prohibited" regulation but modified its enforcement procedure to give a nude person an opportunity to put on a bathing suit before a complaint can be filed or a violation notice issued.

In practical terms, this means that a group at an unposted hot spring can mutually agree to be nude. As soon as anyone else arrives and requests that all present put on bathing suits, those who refuse that request risk a citation. If you are in the nude group, all you need from the newcomers is some tolerance. You may be pleasantly surprised at the number of people who are willing to agree to a policy of clothing-optional if, in a friendly manner, you offer them an opportunity to say "Yes."

Clothing and clothing-optional exist literally side-by-side here at *Loftus Hot Springs*, Idaho.

Carved stone bench at *Ram Creek Hot Spring*.

Ram Creek Hot Spring, Canada, is far enough away from civilization that nude enjoyment of the pools doesn't seem to be a problem at all; in fact, it is encouraged.

Using This Guide

The primary tool in this guide is the KEY MAP, which is provided for each state or geographical sub-division. The KEY MAP INDEX on the outside back cover, tells the page number where each of the KEY MAPS can be found. Each KEY MAP includes significant cities and highways, but please note that it is designed to be used with a standard highway map.

Within every KEY MAP, each location has been assigned a number, that is printed next to the identifying circle or square. On the pages following the KEY MAP you will find the descriptions of each location, listed in numerical order.

The Master Alphabetical Index of Mineral Water Locations is printed at the end of the book, and gives the page number on which each location description will be found. If you know the specific hot spring name, this alphabetical index is the place to start.

The following sections describe the quick-read symbols that are used on the KEY MAPS and in the location descriptions.

A picturesque rock-rimmed pool with gorgeous natural surroundings and a location remote enough for you to be alone, yet not too far from your car, as you soak in water just the right temperature—*St. Martins of the Wind* meets this description of many people's ideal soak.

● **Non-Commercial Mineral Water Locations**

On the key maps and in each hot spring listing, a solid round dot is used to indicate a non-commercial hot spring, or hot well, where no fee is required and pools are generally created by the rearranging of rocks or by using easily available material. At a few remote locations, you may be asked for a donation to help the work of a nonprofit organization that has a contract with the Forest Service to protect and maintain the spring.

The first paragraph of each listing is intended to convey the general appearance, atmosphere, and surroundings of the location, including the altitude, which can greatly affect the weather conditions. The phrase "open all year" does not mean that all roads and trails are kept open regardless of snowfalls or fire seasons. Rather, it means that there are no seasonally closed gates or doors, as at some commercial resorts.

The second paragraph describes the source and temperature of the mineral water and then conveys the manner in which that water is transported or guided to a usable soaking pool. "Volunteer-built pool" usually implies some crude combination of at-hand material such as logs, rocks, and sand. If the situation requires that the pool water temperature be controlled, the method for such control is described. River-edge and creek-edge pools are vulnerable to complete washouts during high runoff months, so often volunteers have to start from scratch every year.

The third paragraph identifies the facilities and services available on the premises or nearby and states the approximate distance to other facilities and services.

If needed, there is a final paragraph of directions, which should be used in connection with a standard highway map, a National Forest map if applicable, or any local area map.

■ Commercial Mineral Water Locations

On the key maps in this book and in the hot springs listings, a solid square is used to indicate a mineral water commercial location. A phone number and address are provided for the purpose of obtaining rates, additional information, and reservations.

The first paragraph of each listing is intended to convey the size, general appearance, atmosphere, and surroundings of the location. "Open all year" does not imply that the facility is open 24 hours of every day, only that it does not have a "closed" season.

The second paragraph of each listing focuses on the water facilities available at the location. It describes the origin and temperature of the mineral water, the means of transporting that water, the quantity, type, and location of tubs and pools, the control of soaking water temperatures, and the chemical treatment used, if any.

In all states, health department standards require a minimum treatment of public pool water with chlorine, bromine, or the equivalent. A few fortunate locations are able to meet these standards by operating their smaller mineral water pools on a continuous flow-through basis, thereby eliminating the need for chemical treatment. Many other locations meet these standards by draining and refilling tubs and pools after each use or after the end of each business day.

Commercial hot springs range from a seasonal communal pool such as this one at *Challis Hot Springs*, Idaho, to an elaborate spa and destination resort such as *The Fairmont* in Canada.

There actually are a few commercial locations where rare geothermal conditions (and health department rules) make it possible to soak in a natural sand-bottom hot spring open to the sky.

At those hot springs resorts that are being run as a business, bathing suits are normally required in public spaces. There are a few locations that have a policy of clothing-optional in the pools and sometimes everywhere on the grounds.

The third paragraph of a commercial hot spring listing briefly mentions the principal facilities and services offered, plus approximate distances to other nearby services and the names of credit cards accepted, if any. This information is intended to advise you if overnight accommodations, RV hookups, restaurants, health clubs, beauty salons, etc., are available on the premises, but it does not attempt to assign any form of quality rating to those amenities. There is no such thing as a typical hot spring resort and no such thing as typical accommodations at such a resort. Don't make assumptions; phone and ask questions.

☐ Tubs Using Gas-heated Tap Water or Well Water

Listings of rent-a-tub locations, indicated by a hollow square, begin with an overall impression of the premises and with the general location, usually within a city area. This is followed by a description of the private spaces, tubs, and pools, water treatment methods, and water temperature policies. Generally, unless stated otherwise, clothing is optional in private spaces and required elsewhere. Facilities and services available on the premises are described. Credit cards accepted, if any, are listed. Nearly all locations require reservations, especially during the busy evening hours.

Nudist/naturist resorts that have hot pools are included as a special service to those who prefer to soak in the buff. It is true that most nudist/naturist resorts are not open to the public for drop-in visits but we wanted to give skinny-dippers at least a few alternatives to the conventional motels/hotels/resorts. Most of the nudist/naturist resorts specifically prohibit bathing suits in their pools and have a policy of clothing optional elsewhere on the grounds. The resorts listed in this book are willing to offer a visitor's pass if you phone ahead and make arrangements.

Kah-Nee-Ta Vacation Resort is a major destination resort on a huge reservation in Oregon. It is owned by the Confederated Tribes of Warm Springs, who have developed the springs into something for everyone, whether you travel in an RV, want to rent a tepee, or prefer to stay at the beautiful lodge.

The hot pool at *Inner City Hot Springs*, in Portland, Oregon, is a typical fiberglass tub, but this location offers many other services that add to the relaxing soak.

Sol Duc Hot Springs Resort, Washington, is the only commercial hot mineral water development in any National Park in the 11 western states.

Caring for the Outdoors

This is an enthusiastic testimonial and an invitation to join us in supporting the work of the US Forest Service, the National Park Service, and the several State Park Services. At all of their offices and ranger stations we have always received prompt, courteous service, even when the staff was also busy handling many other daily tasks.

Nearly all usable primitive hot springs are in national forests, and many commercial hot spring resorts are surrounded by a national forest. Even if you will not be camping in one of their excellent campgrounds, we recommend that you obtain official Forest Service maps for all of the areas through which you will be traveling. Maps may be purchased from the Forest Service Regional Offices listed below. To order by mail, phone or write for an order form:

Rocky Mountain Region   (303) 275-5349
Eastern Wyoming, Colorado
740 Simms St.   Lakewood, CO 80401

Intermountain Region   (801) 625-5352
Southern Idaho, Utah,
Nevada, and Western Wyoming
324 25th St.   Ogden, UT 84401

Pacific Northwest Region
Oregon, Washington
333 SW First Ave.   Portland, OR 97204

Northern Region
Montana, Northern Idaho
PO Box 7669   Missoula, MT 59807

When you arrive at a national forest, head for the nearest ranger station and let them know what you would like to do in addition to putting your body in hot mineral water. If you plan to stay in a wilderness area overnight, request information about the procedure for obtaining wilderness permits and camping permits. Discuss your understanding of the dangers of water pollution, including giardia (back country dysentery) with the Forest Service staff. They are good friends as well as competent public servants.

The following material is adapted from a brochure issued by the Forest Service, Southwestern Region, Department of Agriculture.

DO NOT WASH IN STREAMS OR SPRINGS

Pour wash water on the ground away from streams and springs.

Wash yourself, your dishes and your clothes in a container, away from water sources.

Food scraps, tooth paste, even biodegradable soap will pollute streams and springs. Remember, it's your drinking water, too!

Try to pack out trash left by others. Your good example may catch on!

DON'T SHORT CUT TRAILS.

Trails are designed and maintained to prevent erosion.

PACK IT IN — PACK IT OUT

Bring trash bags to carry out all trash that cannot be completely burned.

Cutting across switchbacks and trampling meadows can create a confusing maze of unsightly trails.

Aluminum foil and aluminum lined packages won't burn up in your fire. Compact it and put it in your trash bag.

CAMPFIRES Use gas stoves when possible to conserve dwindliing supplies of firewood.

Use only fallen timber for firewood. Even standing dead trees are part of the beauty of wilderness, and are important to wildlife.

If you need to build a fire, use an existing campfire site if available.

Clear a circle of all burnable materials.

Dig a shallow pit for the fire.

Keep the sod intact.

If you need to clear a new fire site, select a safe spot away from rock ledges that would be blackened by smoke; away from meadows where it would destroy grass and leave a scar; away from dense brush, trees and duff where it would be a fire hazard. Keep fires small.

Never leave a fire unattended.

Put your fire COLD OUT before leaving, by mixing the coals with dirt & water. Feel it with your hand. If it's cold out, cover the ashes in the pit with dirt, replace the sod, and naturalize the disturbed area. Rockfire rings, if needed or used, should be scattered before leaving.

DON'T BURY TRASH!
Animals dig it up.

BURY HUMAN WASTE

When nature calls, select a suitable spot at least 100 feet from open water, campsites and trails. Dig a hole 4 to 6 inches deep. Try to keep the sod intact.

Don't pick flowers, dig up plants or cut branches from live trees. Leave them for others to see and enjoy.

After use, fill in the hole completely burying waste and TP: then tramp in the sod.

ALASKA

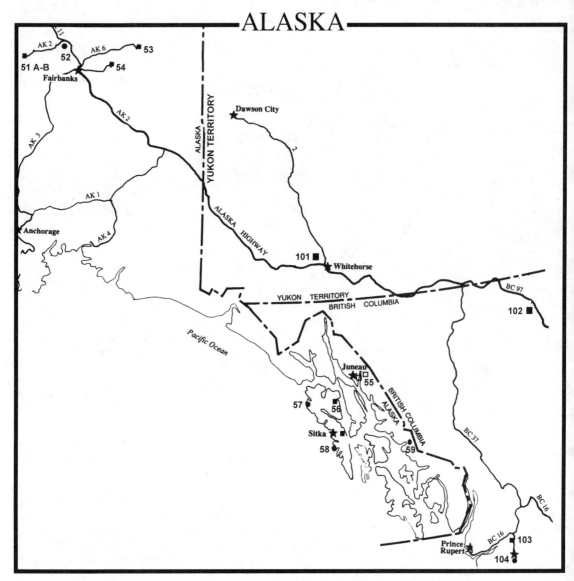

This map was designed to be used with a standard highway map.

MAP SYMBOLS

● Non-commercial mineral water pool
■ Commercial (fee) mineral water pool
□ Gas-heated tap or well water pool

〰〰 Paved highway
– – – Unpaved road
·········· Hiking route

Leaving the end of the quonset hut open enables swimmers to see the trees, lets nature in while keeping cold weather out. The log cabin adds to the rustic feeling and houses the restaurant and bar. Large windows open out onto the forest, and there's a distinct possibility that you will see much of the varied wildlife abundant in the area.

51A   MANLEY HOT SPRINGS RESORT
PO Box 28   (907) 672-3611
■   **Manley Hot Springs, AK 99756**

Rustic lodge with RV park and enclosed mineral water pools, surrounded by birch forests, 160 miles northwest of Fairbanks. Elevation 330 feet. Open all year.

Natural mineral water is pumped out of two drilled wells at 105° and piped to a translucent quonset shelter containing a plastic-lined swimming pool and a fiberglass hydropool. The swimming pool is maintained at 96° and the hydropool is maintained at 104°; both are treated with chlorine. Bathing suits are required.

Lodge rooms, restaurant, bar, RV park, laundromat, gift shop, and gasoline are available on the premises. Geothermal energy is used to heat the buildings. Visa and MasterCard are accepted.

Directions: Drive northwest from Fairbanks on AK 2. The first 28 miles are paved; the remaining 124 miles are a good dirt/gravel road. Phone ahead for winter road conditions. An airstrip is located in the town near the resort.

51B   MANLEY HOT SPRINGS

■   **Manley Hot Springs, AK 99756**

A unique geothermal greenhouse containing four cement soaking tubs in addition to many flowers and organic vegetables. Elevation 330 feet. Open all year.

Natural mineral water flows out of two springs (125° and 136°) and is piped to the greenhouse for space heating and for use in the soaking pools. Temperatures of 80°, 90°, 95°, and 105° are maintained in the four pools, which are drained and refilled each day so no chemical treatment of the water is needed. Bathing suits are required.

While there are no services on the premises, there are comfortable accommodations in Manley, and hunting and fishing are readily available nearby.

Note: This is primarily a commercial greenhouse enterprise, not a rent-a-tub business, so access to the tubs may not always be available. Inquire at the Post Office or at Manley Roadhouse, (907) 672-3161, for current status and directions.

This setting is worth a gratefully accepted donation, which is given to charity, for a chance to soak in these tubs surrounded by hanging baskets of beautiful petunias. Since this is not a commercial hot-tub operation, please be sure to phone first to ensure that the time you have in mind is convenient for the growers.

52   TOLOVANA HOT SPRINGS
■   **PO Box 83058 (907) 455-6706**
       Fairbanks, AK 99708

Two remote and rustic cabins with outdoor cedar soaking tubs surrounded by birch and aspen forests, 100 road miles north of Fairbanks. Elevation: 800 feet. Open all year.

Natural mineral water flows out of many geothermal springs at 135° and collects in a settling pond that maintains a temperature of 100°. Water from each of these two sources is piped to the two widely separated soaking tubs, allowing complete control of tub water temperature. The apparent local custom is clothing optional.

The two fully outfitted cabins are the only services available on the premises. There is a remote air strip two miles from the cabins, and it is 11 miles by all-year trail to the nearest road. It is 35 miles to a phone, gas, and an air strip at Minto Village. Local air charters are available. Phone for guided dog sled, snow-machine, or ski trips. Phone for rates, reservations, and weather conditions. No credit cards are accepted.

While a soak surrounded by nature's winter wonderland is magical, it would be wise to heed the words in the Tolovana Hot Springs brochure: "The trails to Tolovana Hot Springs are for the adventurous. Experience is recommended for winter travel." Even in summer it is still and 11-mile hike, unless, of course, you charter a plane and fly in. Then the hike is only two miles.

While the tubs in summer don't look quite as magical as in winter, you are still surrounded by beautiful trees and a peaceful atmosphere.

The original hotel was built in 1930 with building materials floated down the Yukon River or hauled overland by wagon. The rooms in the hotel have been refurbished to reflect the early 1900s. The cabins with private hydropools were built sometime later.

According to all the travel literature, *Chena Hot Springs* is the ideal place to relax after viewing the "midnight Sun" at the summer solstice in June. Located in what was once gold country, there are also many other things to do in the area during the rest of the year.

53	CIRCLE HOT SPRINGS	
	PO Box 254	(907) 520-5113
■	Central, AK 99730	

Delightful historic resort hotel and cabins with a large outdoor swimming pool and several private-space hydropools, 134 miles northeast of Fairbanks. Elevation 900 feet. Open all year.

Natural mineral water flows out of a spring at 139° and is piped to an outdoor Olympic-size swimming pool and to individual hydropools in four cabins, one hydropool in the honeymoon suite and one hydropool on each of the three main floors of the hotel. The swimming pool is maintained at 105°, with a minimum of chlorination. Day use is available in the swimming pool and in the three main-floor hydropools. Bathing suits are required in the swimming pool.

Hotel rooms, dining room, saloon, and library are available on the premises. Geothermal energy is used to heat all rooms and cabins. All types of hunting and fishing are located nearby and tours can be arranged. It is eight miles to all other services in Central. No credit cards are accepted.

Directions: From Fairbanks, drive north on Steese Highway, then east on AK 6 to Central, and east for 8 miles on Hot Springs Road to the resort. Phone for information on rates, reservations, and road conditions in winter.

54	CHENA HOT SPRINGS	
	PO Box 73440	(907) 452-7867
■	Fairbanks, AK 99707	

Comfortable lodge with cabins, an indoor swimming pool, a soaking pool, and two whirlpools. Located in a wooded valley 57 miles east of Fairbanks. Elevation 1,200 feet. Open all year.

Natural mineral water flows out of four springs at temperatures up to 156° and is piped to several pools that are treated with chlorine. The glassed-in swimming pool is maintained at 90°; the indoor soaking pool is maintained at 104°; and the two indoor whirlpools are maintained at 100°. The new pool building includes a deck containing an outdoor hydrojet pool that is maintained at 104°. All pools are available for day use as well as for registered guests. Bathing suits are required.

Hotel rooms, cabins, RV hookups (electricity, dump station), laundry, restaurant, and bar are available on the premises. Activities on the grounds include horseback riding, cross-country skiing, snowmobiling, sledding, fishing, badminton, horseshoes, volleyball, and hiking. It is 57 miles to all other services in Fairbanks. Visa, MasterCard and American Express are accepted.

Directions: From Fairbanks, follow Chena Hot Springs Road (paved) east to the resort. Phone for rates and reservations.

Originally built in 1913, this oldest operating hotel and bar in Juneau has recently been listed in the National Register of Historic Sites and has been refurbished with oak antiques, brass, and stained glass. Hot tubs are for rent in the basement under the name "Juneau Hot Springs."

55   THE ALASKAN HOTEL
167 S. Franklin St.(800) 327-9374
☐   Juneau, AK 99801

Hourly hot tub and sauna rentals in an historic downtown Juneau hotel. Elevation 20 feet. Open all year.

Four private-space hot pools, using electrically heated tap water treated with bromine, are available for rent to the public as well as for use by registered hotel guests. Water temperature is maintained at 101°, and each space includes a sauna. The three smaller tubs will hold four persons; the larger one will hold six. Clothing is optional within the private spaces.

Rooms and a bar are available on the premises. All other services are available in the surrounding city of Juneau. Visa, MasterCard, American Express and Discover are accepted.

The hotel is located in the South Franklin Historic District. Phone for rates, reservations, and directions.

56   TENAKEE HOT SPRINGS

■   In the town of Tenakee Springs
A wooden bathhouse containing a concrete soaking pool, built over a hot spring in a tiny rural Alaskan village with no cars or roads. Elevation is sea level. Open all year.

Natural mineral water flows out of the spring at 108°, directly up into a five-foot by ten-foot concrete container that was built to keep out the sea water at high tide. Men and women are assigned different hours of the day. Bathing suits and soap are prohibited in the pool. Donations are accepted in the adjoining store.

There are no services available on the premises, but rooms, bunkhouse, bar, and laundry are offered nearby in the nostalgic Victorian Tenakee Inn, (800) 327-9347. A restaurant and curio shop are located nearby.

The Alaska Marine Highway Ferry stops for only 15 minutes at Tenakee Springs, which is located on the north shore of Tenakee Inlet on Chichagof Island, 45 miles southwest of Juneau.

Tenakee Hot Springs is the main attraction in a town with no cars and single gravel street. The wooden bathhouse has separate hours set aside for men and women throughout the day.

57 WHITE SULPHUR HOT SPRINGS

● **Northwest of the city of Sitka**

Remote hot spring pools with a nearby rentable National Forest Service cabin, within a beautiful wilderness area of Tongass National Forest, 65 miles from Sitka. Elevation 50 feet. Open all year.

Natural mineral water flows out of one spring at 111°, supplying a natural-bottom primitive soaking pool. A three-sided log structure with a concrete soaking pool has been built directly over another spring. The open side of this shelter provides a spectacular view of Pacific Ocean waves crashing on rocky cliffs. The apparent local clothing custom is the mutual agreement of those present.

There are no services available on the premises, but camping is available on open wilderness land. Access is only by boat, plus a one-mile hike from Mirror Harbor. For cabin reservation information, charter boat rental, and a detailed map to the springs, contact the US Forest Service, 204 Siginaka Way, Sitka, AK 99835. (907) 747-6671.

While you sit in this tranquil outside pool at *White Sulphur Hot Springs*, it is possible to see the often turbulent Pacific Ocean.

58 GODDARD HOT SPRINGS

● **South of the city of Sitka**

Two modern cedar soaking tubs in open shelters overlooking beautiful Hot Springs Bay and located on City of Sitka land on the outer coast of Baranof Island. Elevation 30 feet. Open all year.

Natural mineral water flows out of a spring at 153° and is piped to a double faucet on each tub. Cold water is also piped to that faucet, permitting complete control of the tub water temperature. There is no charge for using the facilities, which are owned and maintained by the City of Sitka. The apparent local clothing custom is the mutual agreement of those present.

Boardwalks and stairs have been constructed and camping is permitted in the open spaces, although the usual dampness of the area can make for uncomfortable camping. There are no other services available on the premises. Access is possible only by charter boat. For more information, contact the Sitka Convention and Visitors Bureau, PO Box 1226 Sitka, AK 99835. (907) 747-5940.

Goddard Hot Springs provides a beautiful view of peaceful Hot Springs Bay. The walkways and stairs put in by the City of Sitka provide access to the tubs.

● **North of the community of Wrangell**

Located along the base of a steep, glaciated, granite cliff surrounded by willow and stands of Sitka spruce and hemlock, within the Tongass National Forest. Elevation 25 feet. Recommended June to October.

Natural mineral water emerges from beneath boulders at the base of a cliff at approximately 120° and is piped to a large wooden tub enclosed in a post-and-beam style structure with insect screening. The other tub is in an open structure overlooking a meadow. The apparent local clothing custom is the mutual agreement of those present. There is considerable local traffic evenings and weekends, so please use discretion and whatever you pack in, pack out.

Changing rooms, benches, and outdoor privies are available on the premises. The nearest public recreation cabins (reservations required) are within three miles. All other services are in Wrangell or Telegraph Creek, BC.

Access is by boat via Hot Springs Slough, a tributary of Ketili Slough, a side channel of the Stikine River, 28 miles from Wrangell. Ease of access depends on river level; during low levels, access by watercraft may be limited. It is also possible to fly into Telegraph Creek, BC, and to kayak or motor boat down to the river's mouth. While the rapids are not difficult, there is much submerged material in the river, making it a challenge for beginners. It is recommended that you follow someone down the river the first time and travel with several spare props and a pole. For cabin reservations, charter flights, boat rental information, and detailed directions to the spring, contact the US Forest Service, Tongass National forest, Wrangell Ranger District, PO Box 51, Wrangell, AK 99929; (907) 874-2323. They also have maps and printed information of the area.

Source map: USGS *Petersburg C-1* topographic map. (The hot springs actually lie about 1.86 miles due east of the position shown on the map.)

Dating back to aboriginal times, this site was more recently developed by local citizens for their own use and is currently maintained by the National Forest Service. The trail to the springs begins at the low-water landing and, after a series of log staircases and a log stringer bridge, connects the upper, enclosed tub with the open-air structure below and then continues down to the high-water landing. Along with hot springs enthusiasts, black and brown bears, moose, wolf, and waterfowl inhabit the area.

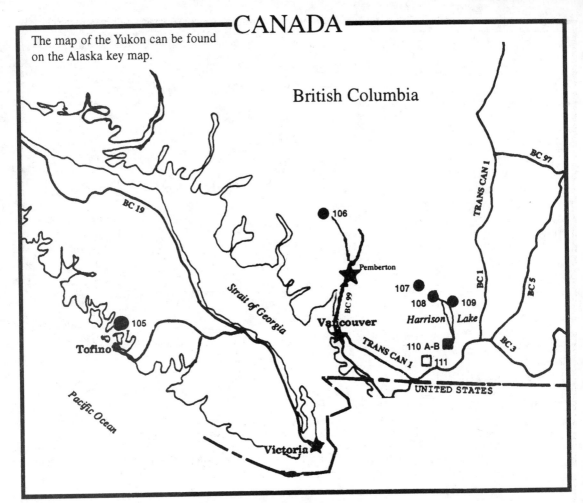

CANADA

The map of the Yukon can be found on the Alaska key map.

British Columbia

BC 19

BC 97

TRANS CAN 1

● 106

Pemberton ★

BC 99

107 ●

108 ● ● 109

BC 1

BC 5

● 105

Strait of Georgia

Vancouver

Harrison Lake

110 A-B ■

□ 111

BC 3

Tofino

TRANS CAN 1

Pacific Ocean

UNITED STATES

Victoria ★

This map was designed to be used with a standard highway map.

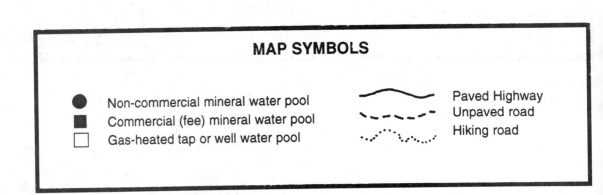

MAP SYMBOLS

● Non-commercial mineral water pool
■ Commercial (fee) mineral water pool
□ Gas-heated tap or well water pool

Paved Highway
Unpaved road
Hiking road

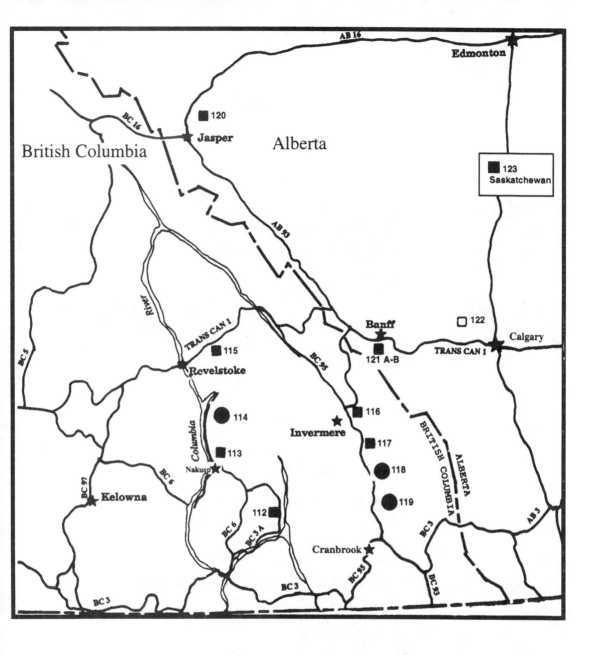

British Columbia

Alberta

Edmonton

Jasper

■ 120

■ 123
Saskatchewan

AB 16

BC 16

AB 93

River

TRANS CAN 1

BC 5

■ 115

Revelstoke

● 114

Columbia

BC 95

Banff

■ 121 A-B

□ 122

Calgary

TRANS CAN 1

■ 116

● Invermere

■ 117

● 118

■ 113

Nakusp

BC 97

BC 6

Kelowna

● 119

BRITISH COLUMBIA

ALBERTA

■ 112

BC 6

BC 3 A

Cranbrook

BC 3

AB 3

BC 3

BC 95

BC 33

BC 3

After a long horseback ride (horses are available for rent at the resort), both the sign and the pool at *Takhini Hot Springs* are a welcoming site. Early trappers gained access to these springs, which were formed by volcanic action, via the old Dawson Trail or by the Takhini River.

101   TAKHINI HOT SPRINGS
(shown on the Alaska key map)
RR #2, Site 19, Comp 4 (403) 633-2706
■   **Whitehorse, Yukon, Y1A 5A5**

Restaurant, campground, and mineral water pool in the scenic Takhini River valley. Daylight lasts from 19 hours in June to 5 1/2 hours in December. Elevation 2,400 feet. Open all year, but closed most weekdays from October 1 to February 28.

Natural mineral water flows out of a spring at 118° and is piped to a large outdoor pool, where it is mixed with cold water as needed to maintain a temperature of 102-104°. The pool is drained and refilled each day, so a minimum of chlorination is needed. Bathing suits are required.

Restaurant, RV and tent campground, sauna, showers, laundromat, and horseback riding are available on the premises. It is 17 miles to all other services in Whitehorse. No credit cards are accepted.

Directions: Northwest of Whitehorse on the Alaska Highway, turn north on YT 2 toward Dawson City. Drive 3 miles, then watch for the Takhini Hot Springs sign and turn west 6 miles to the springs.

Liard Hot Springs: A beautiful provincial park on the Alaska Highway with a six-foot-wide boardwalk wandering through a wetlands environment where you are likely to view over 250 boreal forest plants—several supported by the hot springs conditions. Wildlife is also prevelant. The Beta pool (above) provides a hot, deep soak and a swim.

102   LIARD HOT SPRINGS PROVINCIAL PARK
(shown on the Alaska key map)
■   **Northwest of Muncho Lake, BC**

A lovely, primitive geothermal pond and pool with convenient boardwalk access and a campground, adjoining the Alaska Highway near the Yukon border. Elevation 1,500 feet. Open all year.

Natural mineral water flows out of several springs at temperatures up to 120° directly into a large, shallow, natural pond (named Alpha) created by a low dam across the creek bed. The water cools to comfortable levels as it flows toward the spillway over the dam. Underwater benches are provided for soaking, and the shallow end of the pond is suitable for children. One side of the pond has been improved with stairs, a large deck, changing rooms, and toilets. A six-foot-wide boardwalk has been built through a wetlands environment from the parking area to the pond. Bathing suits are required.

Five minutes beyond Alpha, along a dirt path, is a large natural pool (named Beta) that maintains a temperature of more than 100°. It also has stairs, a small deck, changing rooms, and toilets, but it is used primarily by adults because of the deep water.

There is no charge for day use of the pools, but a fee is charged for sites in the campground. During the popular summer months, campsites fill early in the day. There are no other services available on the premises. There is a cafe across the highway and a lodge within .5 miles. It is 41 miles to all other services. No credit cards are accepted.

The park is located at mile marker 497 (765 km) on the Alaska Highway (BC 97) just below the Yukon Territory border. Follow the signs prominently displayed along the highway.

The dam pictured on the left creates the shallow Alpha pond that is ideal for children and soakers. Underwater benches are comfortable, and waterfalls are unique.

103 MOUNT LAYTON HOT SPRINGS RESORT
(shown on the Alaska key map)
PO Box 550   (604) 798-2214
■   Terrace, BC V8G 4B5

A large, new 1,000-acre destination resort and water park in a beautiful setting on the edge of Lakelse Lake in Western British Columbia. Elevation 800 feet. Open all year.

Natural mineral water flows out of several springs at temperatures up to 186°, is treated with ozone, and is then piped to various pools and waterslides without requiring any other chemical treatment. The outdoor therapeutic pool is maintained at 103° and the outdoor main pool is maintained at 90°. Two of the three big waterslides exit into an indoor catch pool that is maintained at 90°. The third big waterslide exits outdoors into an arm of the main pool. There are also two short outdoor waterslides suitable for small children. Bathing suits are required.

Hotel rooms, restaurant, bar, and snack room are available on the premises. Fishing and boating are available at adjoining Lakelse Lake. It is 10 miles to all other services in Terrace. Visa, MasterCard, Diners, and American Express are accepted.

Directions: From Terrace, drive 14 miles south on BC 37 to the resort.

Mount Layton: Three different waterslides can be reached in this tower. Children too small for these big slides have two slides of their own in the shallow end.

Two of the *Mount Layton* waterslides have an indoor catch pool so that fun can continue no matter what the outdoor weather is like.

104 DOUGLAS CHANNEL HOT SPRINGS
●   (shown on the Alaska key map)

Eight different natural hot spring sites, some partially improved, along the edges of beautiful Douglas Channel. Accessible only by boat. Elevation sea level. Open all year.

The following three sites are the most popular.

Bishop Bay: One spring, 110°, 15 feet above high tide, supplies a three-foot by three-foot concrete bathhouse. Mooring buoys and a dock are in place.

Weewanie: One spring, 117°, 330 feet above sea level, supplies a small cement bathhouse, built with a grant from Crown Zellerbach.

Shearwater Point: Several springs, 113°, in a fractured rock wall supply a brick pool built by a lumber company for its employees in 1922.

The other sites are difficult to find and/or are flooded at high tide. For more information, contact the Kitimat Chamber of Commerce, PO Box 214, Kitimat, BC V8C 2G7. (604) 632-6294, FAX (604) 632-4685.

Directions: Kitimat is at the head of Douglas Channel, 36 miles south of Terrace on BC 37.

After an easy walk from the dock, it becomes a scramble to get to all the different small pools located up the channel. Whether it's a soak or a shower you want, there is plenty of hot water at the several places along the cliffs where the water cascades over the sides.

Northwest of the town of Tofino,
● on Vancouver Island

Unique confluence of geothermal runoff and ocean waves, located in Maquinna Regional Park on a rocky peninsula reachable only by boat or float-plane. Elevation 40 feet. Open all year.

Natural mineral water flows out of the main spring at 122°, providing a hot showerbath as it falls over a cliff edge. This geothermal water gradually cools as it flows through a series of soaking pools in a rocky channel leading to the ocean. The incoming tide and wave action intermittently splash cold sea water over the visitors in the lower pools. Clothing optional is the apparent local custom. The remoteness of this location does not assure you of privacy. During summer weekends, you will have plenty of company, which insures a maximum of excitement when the icy waves surge into the tubs.

There are no facilities or services on the premises. It is one mile on a cedar-board walk to a fishing-boat dock with a quaint small store that is usually open for snacks, soft drinks, etc. Overnight camping near the springs is not prohibited. Rooms are available in the lodge at a nearby Indian village.

For information and reservations, contact Tofino Adventures Booking Centre, Box 620., Tofino, BC VOR 2Z0. (604) 725 4222. You might want to inquire about whale-watching trips, kayak adventures, and sailing cruises.

106   MEAGER CREEK HOT SPRINGS

● **North of the town of Pemberton**

The largest and most active geothermal area in British Columbia, surrounded by wild rivers, creeks, multiple sources of hot water, and volcanic remains. Open all year, road conditions permitting; check in Pemberton.

Water sources ranging from 100-200° (watch where you walk) fill two large wooden tubs. The water in the two tubs can be regulated by diverting hotter or cooler source water via pipes. Also, several rock pools of various sizes and temperatures are located near various spring outlets and along the creek. Well-built boardwalks and stairs connect all the springs and pools. Clothing optional seems to be the local custom.

There are outhouses and picnic tables on the premises. The nearest campground and all services are in Pemberton, 40 miles south.

Directions: From the town of Pemberton, go north on the Lillooet Forest Road for 14.4 miles, then cross a bridge over the Lillooet River. You will then pass the Coast Mountain Outdoor School. Continue north on the forest road for 24 miles to the junction of Meager Creek and the Lillooet River. Cross the bridge over the river and head southwest for 3.8 miles to a fork in the road. Keep left and continue for 1.4 miles, then cross over the Meager Creek bridge. There is a large parking area located here, as well as a large sign/map showing the various paths to the pools.

Boardwalks and stairs connect both the wooden tubs and the several rock pools along the creek. Bring a picnic and spend the day trying all the different pools.

A great deal of piping is necessary to bring both hot and cold water to these tubs to adjust them to an absolutely perfect soaking temperature. After the rough road in, a soak really feels good.

The best thing about this A-frame is that it could be used to attach mosquito netting—sometimes greatly needed.

107 SKOOKUMCHUCK HOT SPRINGS (LILLOOET) (ST. AGNES WELL)
● **South of the town of Pemberton, BC**

Two large, fiberglass soaking tubs in a small clearing near a logging road along the Lillooet River. Elevation 100 feet. Open all year; however, the road is not plowed in winter.

Natural mineral water flows out of a spring at 129°. Volunteers have mounted the two halves of a fiberglass storage tank near the springs, using long pieces of PVC pipe to bring a gravity flow of hot mineral water. Other pieces of PVC pipe are used to carry a gravity flow from a cold-water spring. Water temperature within each tub is controlled by mixing the hot and cold water. One of the tubs is in the open; the other is under a crude A-frame shelter. In the absence of posted rules, the use of bathing suits is determined by the consent of those present.

There are no services available, but there are numerous nearby self-maintained camping areas along the logging road and at the site itself.

Directions: From the town of Mt. Currie, go approximately 34 miles on a rough logging road along the Lillooet River. At BC Hydro tower #682, turn right onto a camping-area access road and go .25 miles to spring. Caution: This dirt road may require a four-wheel-drive vehicle when wet.

The hot springs are located on private property, and use is permissible without the consent of the property owner. Please respect the hot springs and adjacent property. Pack out all garbage.

108 SLOQUET CREEK HOT SPRINGS

● **Near the north end of Harrison Lake, BC**

These hot springs are located about 62 miles south of Mt. Currie, near the Lillooet River and just northwest of Harrison Lake. Elevation approximately 1000 feet. Open all year, weather permitting.

Water comes out of the springs at temperatures from 135-155°. Several springs seep from the rocks around Sloquet Creek and flow along the ground before dropping over a short waterfall and forming a small pool that is too hot for bathing. Several other springs percolate from the ground, and volunteers have constructed small, natural-rock pools for bathing along the creek.

Few services are available in the area, though there is a logging camp at Port Douglas, at the head of Harrison Lake. Walk-in camping is possible near the springs.

Directions: From the town of Mt. Currie, go about 57 miles south on the logging road along the Lillooet River to a bridge that crosses the river to the west side. Turn left, cross Fire Creek, and go south two miles to a second creek, where you go right. Follow this creek (Sloquet) for about 3.4 miles on an old logging road that takes you to a bridge across North Sloquet Creek. The bridge is washed out and you must cross the creek on foot via a large log. Follow the logging road until you reach an obvious clearing that can be used for camping. There is a trail leading downhill from the clearing to the creek and the hot springs. It will take two to three hours to drive from Mt. Currie and an additional 45 minutes to walk the remainder of the logging road to the hot springs. There are no posted rules or regulations for use of the site, but anything packed in should be packed out, including garbage.

109 CLEAR CREEK HOT SPRINGS
Along the northeast side
● **of Harrison Lake, BC**

Two small wooden tubs and two old porcelain bathtubs are located near a log cabin along Clear Creek, approximately 35 miles up the east side of Harrison Lake from Harris Hot Springs, and six miles east of the lake up Clear Creek. Elevation approximately 2,200 feet. Hot springs open all year; however, road is passable only in summer and only by four-wheel-drive vehicles.

A spring percolates from the ground at 95°, and volunteers have constructed two wooden tubs connected to the springs with long lengths of PVC pipe. There are two conventional bathtubs that can also be used for soaking.

There are few amenities available in the area other than the log cabin and an outhouse nearby. The springs are located on an active mineral claim that was initially prospected by a woman who built the cabin and an Olympic-size swimming pool about 15 years ago. The pool is largely filled with algae and silt and no longer used by bathers.

Directions: From the town of Harrison Hot Springs, head up the east side of Harrison Lake for about 33 miles to the logging camp at Big Silver Creek. Stay on the main logging road for another five miles and look for a narrow road going off to the right. This is the old mining road up Clear Creek, and it is extremely rough in places. It is driveable with a narrow, four-wheel-drive vehicle for most of the six miles to the hot springs and cabin, which are located on the right side of the creek. It will take two to three hours to drive from Harrison Hot Springs to the Clear Creek road, and considerably longer if you walk up the road. There are no posted rules, but anything packed in should be packed out, including garbage.

110A THE HARRISON HOTEL
(604) 521-8888
■ Harrison Hot Springs, BC V0M 1K0

Attractive, large destination resort located on the south shore of beautiful Lake Harrison, 65 miles east of Vancouver. This well-managed facility offers an unusually wide range of recreational activities. Elevation 47 feet. Open all year.

Natural mineral water flows out of a spring at 140° and is piped to cooling tanks before being treated with chlorine. The Olympic-size outdoor swimming pool is maintained at 82°, the indoor swimming pool at 94°, and the indoor soaking pool at 104°. The men's and women's sections of the health pavilion each contain a Roman bath in which the temperature is controllable. Health pavilion services are available to the public, but all other facilities are reserved for registered guests only. Bathing suits are required.

Future development plans include four large outdoor soaking pools with connecting waterfalls and temperatures ranging from 110° down to 85°, two outdoor chlorine-treated fresh water swimming pools ranging in temperature from 78-82°, and a swimway connecting the indoor swimming pool with the outdoor swimming pool. Plans for the health pavilion include mud baths, fitness center and weight room, herbal wraps, etc. Phone ahead to determine the status of construction.

A restaurant, bungalows, rooms, children's programs, pickle ball, boat cruises, and boat rentals are available on the premises. All major credit cards are accepted. Phone for rates, reservations, and additional directions.

110B HARRISON HOT SPRINGS PUBLIC POOL
c/o Harrison Hotel
■ Harrison Hot Springs, BC V0M 1K0

Large, modern, indoor communal plunge owned and operated by the hotel, available to the public. Elevation 47 feet. Open all year.

Natural mineral water drawn from the same spring that supplies the hotel is treated with chlorine and maintained at 100°. Bathing suits are required.

Locker rooms are available on the premises. All other services are within three blocks. Visa and MasterCard are accepted.

Location: On the main intersection at the beach in Harrison Hot Springs.

111 SUNNY TRAILS CLUB
Box 18, 43955 #7 Highway (604) 826-3419
□ Lake Errock, BC V0M 1N0

Located amid old growth cedars, maples, and firs in a natural wilderness area. Elevation 700 feet. Open all year.

Two pools offering spectacular views use spring water from the forest reserve. The enclosed hydropool is maintained at 104°. The outdoor swimming pool is unheated, and both pools are treated with chlorine. Bathing suits are prohibited in the pools and sauna.

Facilities include a cafe, playground, tent sites, RV hookups, clubhouse with rec room and "hotel" rooms, and laundry facilities. It is one mile to a store/service station. No credit cards are accepted.

Note: This is a membership nudist organization and only INF members have unlimited access. Nonmembers may have daytime visits but no overnight privileges. Phone or write for information.

112   AINSWORTH HOT SPRINGS
PO Box 1268   (604) 229-4212
(800) 668-1171
■   **Ainsworth Hot Springs BC V0G 1A0**

Modern, all-year destination resort with a multi-pool plunge and geothermal caves, overlooking beautiful Kootenay Lake. Elevation 1,900 feet. Open all year.

Natural mineral water flows out of five springs at temperatures ranging from 110-117°. The outdoor swimming pool and connected hydrojet pool are maintained at 85-95°. The water in the caves ranges from 106-110° and is circulated to the connected outdoor soaking pool, where it ranges from 104-106°. There is a ledge in the cave that may be used as a steambath. There is also an outdoor cold pool containing creek water ranging from 40-60°. All pools are treated with chlorine. Bathing suits are required.

Facilities include hotel rooms, lounge, dining room, banquet rooms, meeting rooms and dressing rooms. Massage, by appointment, is available on the premises. It is .5 miles to overnight camping and nine miles to a store and service station. MasterCard, Visa and Diners Club are accepted.

Location: On BC 31, 12 miles south of Kaslo and 29 miles from Nelson.

For those who like extremes, a soak in the hot, steamy caves followed by a dip in the cold pool would be the perfect combination.

Nearby camping or a stay in the hotel would make for a wonderful vacation with access to these beautiful pools and a mineral-water cave, something very unusual to tell your friends about when you get home.

113   NAKUSP HOT SPRINGS
PO Box 280   (604) 265-4528
■   Nakusp, BC V0G 1R0

Modern, clean, city-owned plunge with creekside camping spaces surrounded by beautiful mountain scenery. Elevation 2,200 feet. Open all year.

Natural mineral water flows out of springs at 135° and is piped to two outdoor pools where it is treated with chlorine. The swimming pool is maintained at 100° and the soaking pool at 110°. Bathing suits are required.

Locker rooms, cabins and overnight camping, cross-country skiing, hiking trails, and creek fishing are available on the premises. It is eight miles to a cafe, store, service station, and RV hookups. Visa cards are accepted.

Directions: From a junction on BC 23 one mile north of Nakusp, follow signs eight miles east to the plunge.

In summer or winter the view from *Halcyon Hot Springs* to the Arrow Lake valley and the Monashee Mountain range is spectacular. A special thank-you is owed to the owner of these springs for being kind enough to give his permission to use these tubs. A good way to say "you're welcome," is to keep the area clean.

114   HALCYON HOT SPRINGS
●   North of the town of Nakusp

Two tubs with a 30-mile view up and down the Arrow Lake valley and of the surrounding Monashee Mountain range. Elevation 1,900 feet. Open all year; only 400 yards from the highway but roads are very slippery in winter.

Natural mineral water at 120° flows out of the hillside approximately 150 feet above the pools into a small concrete catch basin and down the hill, cooling as it reaches the two pools. The upper pool is wooden, nine by fifteen feet and 1.5 feet deep. The lower pool is fed by a pipe from the upper pool and measures six by six feet and 3.5 feet deep, about the same as a hot tub. The temperatures in the tubs range from 100-108°, depending on flow (which can be adjusted by pipes) and air temperature. The apparent local custom is clothing optional. The site is located on private land, so please keep it very clean.

There are no services on the premises. The nearest campground and all services are in Nakusp, 21 miles away.

Directions: Go exactly 21 miles north of downtown Nakusp on Hwy 23 and start looking for a steep dirt road filled with potholes that veers off almost parallel to the highway on the right (east) side. Travel approximately 300 yards up this road (only in summer). There will be three or four switchbacks (or tiers) to the right. Park on any of these tiers or switchbacks. The springs are located on the second tier, about 75 yards in. In winter or very slippery conditions, do not attempt to drive up unless you have a suitably equipped vehicle. If you park off the highway it is only a 400-yard walk uphill (you will be able to see the column of steam emanating from the springs).

Source map: *Arrow Lakes Forest District Recreation Map* (BC Forest Service). Phone: 604-365-2131.

Canyon Hot Springs: Another springs surrounded by a gorgeous view of the Monashee Mountains.

115 CANYON HOT SPRINGS
PO Box 2400 (604) 837-2420
■ **Revelstoke, BC V0E 2S0**

Well-kept commercial plunge with creekside camping spaces and a spectacular view of the Monashee mountain range. Elevation 3,000 feet. Open May 15 to September 15.

Natural mineral water is piped from Alberet Canon Spring at 85° and is gas-heated, as needed, and treated with chlorine. The outdoor swimming pool is maintained at 85° and the outdoor soaking pool at 105°. Bathing suits are required.

Locker rooms, cafe, store, RV hookups and overnight camping are available on the premises. It is 23 miles to a service station and motel in Revelstoke. Visa, MasterCard, and American Express are accepted.

Location: 23 miles east of Revelstoke on Canada 1.

Although campsites don't have quite the view of *Radium Hot Springs* that the hotel has, there are several campgrounds in the vicinity to use while enjoying the pools.

116 RADIUM HOT SPRINGS
PO Box 220 (604) 347-9485
(800) 767-1611
■ **Radium Hot Springs, BC V0A 1M0**

A modern, clean, and proper Canadian Parks Service communal plunge with adjoining commercial services, surrounded by the beautiful mountain scenery of Kootenay National Park. Elevation 2,800 feet. Open all year.

Natural mineral water flows out of several springs that are underneath and along the northeast wall of the hot pool and is collected and redistributed throughout the complex.at a combined temperature of 114°. It is piped to two outdoor pools, where it is treated with chlorine. The swimming pool is maintained at a temperature of 85°, and the soaking pool is maintained at a temperature of 102°. The pool complex is fully wheelchair accessible. Bathing suits are required.

Locker rooms, bathing suit and towel rentals, massage, and a cafe are available on the premises along with a restaurant, hotel, and motel. The government campground is located on a plateau above the pool complex, and a short trail leads to the pool. It is 1.5 miles to a store and service station in Radium. No credit cards are accepted.

Directions: Follow signs one mile east from the West Gate of Kootenay National Park.

The mineral content of the water at *Radium Hot Springs* is quite similar to the world famous sulphur springs at Bath, England, and other well-known European spas.

117 FAIRMONT HOT SPRINGS RESORT
   PO Box 10   (604) 345-6311
■ **Fairmont Hot Springs, BC V0B 1L0**

Famous, large destination resort and communal plunge, located at the headwaters of the mighty Columbia River, beautifully landscaped and surrounded by the forested mountains of the Windermere Valley. Elevation 2,100 feet. Open all year.

Natural mineral water flows out of three springs at temperatures of 108°, 112°, and 116° and is piped to the resort pools, where it is treated with chlorine and cooled with creek water as needed. The outdoor public plunge area includes a swimming pool maintained at 93°, a soaking pool maintained at 105°, an indoor soaking pool is maintained at 106° and reserved for hotel guests only, and a diving plunge maintained at 90°. Bathing suits are required.

Locker rooms, massage, restaurants, conference center, spa services, store, service station, hotel rooms, full-service RV hookups, saddle horses, tennis, and golf are available on the premises with river rafting, skiing, and other seasonal sports nearby. Major credit cards are accepted.

Location: On BC 93, 64 miles north of Cranbrook and 100 miles south of Banff. The resort also has a private airport.

The Kootenai, Shuswap, and Blackfoot Indians were the first to use the hot springs around Fairmont. The land was homesteaded in 1887, and in 1888 a rest stop for stagecoaches was built. The first "resort" was built in the early 1900s, and in 1957 two brothers bought Fairmont and expanded the pools. One of the brothers still owns the resort and has developed it into what you see today.

118   LUSSIER HOT SPRINGS

● **South of the village of Canal Flats**

A covered staircase leads part of the way down a steep, bare embankment to the pools, which are located on the banks of the Lussier River in the East Kootenays in Southeastern British Columbia. Elevation 3800 feet. Open all year.

Natural mineral water flows out at 110° into the uppermost wooden pool five by three feet and two feet deep. The second pool with a gravel bottom and rock walls is 12 feet in diameter and about 1.5 feet deep. The third pool is 10 feet in diameter and about two feet deep. The water in the third pool can be adjusted by diverting water from a small cold spring into the pool. A good way to cool off is to just step out of the pools and into the river, but watch out for kayackers! The two lowest pools, about eight feet square and 1.5 feet deep, are usually flooded out during all but the driest part of the year (watch for glass in the bottom of these pools). Water temperatures starting at 110° decrease in each pool down the line.

There is a small changing room and garbage cans in the parking area and fresh cold water from the river. The nearest campground is approximately three miles east on the same road. A small store is located in Canal Flats, and the nearest gas station and lodgings are to be found in Fairmont, 20 miles north on Hwy 93.

Directions: From the village of Canal Flats, head south on Hwy 93 for three miles to a well-marked turnoff on the east side of the highway to Whiteswan Lake Provincial Park. Follow this road (Whiteswan forestry road) for 11.5 miles. The springs are well marked on the south (right) side of the road (the large sign on the north side indicates the beginning of Whiteswan Lake Provincial Park). As this road is quite busy all year round with logging trucks and mining trucks hauling ore, please drive with your headlights on.

Source map: *Invermere Forest District Map* (BC Forest Service). Phone: 604-342-4200.

Stepping into the river from one of these pools is a great way to cool off. Warning! Watch out for boaters.

119   RAM CREEK HOT SPRINGS

● **Between Fairmont and Cranbrook**

Three rock pools located in a ravine halfway up the side of a mountain in the East Kootenays, with a fantastic view and with temperatures perfect for all-day soaking. Also a very good place to view the hummingbirds that frequent the area, but do watch out for spots of poison oak. Elevation 4,800 feet. Open mid-May to mid-November, for those with sturdy cars; any other time can be very dangerous.

Three gravel-bottom, rock-wall pools about two feet deep are each fed by individual springs with temperatures at 96° in the upper pool, 93° in the middle pool, and 88° in the lower pool. The apparent local custom is clothing optional.

There are no facilities on the premises. Drinking water is available from a stream one mile back down the road. The nearest campground is located in Premier Lake Provincial Park, 8.5 miles back down the road you just came up. The closest gas station is in Skookumchuck, .5 mile south of the turnoff from Hwy 93. Lodging and other amenities can be found in Cranbrook, 45 miles south on Hwy 93, or in Invermere, 60 miles north on Hwy 93.

Directions: From the town of Canal Flats go south on Hwy 93 for 17 miles to a well-marked turnoff to Premier Lake Provincial Park on the (left) east side of the highway. From this turnoff (consider this point 0), proceed east 4.3 miles to a T intersection.

Do not turn right (south) here. This is the turnoff to Premier Lake. Turn left (north) on what is now known as Sheep Creek Road. At 5.3 miles, the paved road crosses a river via a sturdy wooden bridge and passes two farms. At 5.8 miles, the paved road ends and is now called White/Ram Forest Road. Turn on your headlights and slowly proceed up this dirt road to mile 12.8. Park your car on the north (left) side of th road. The springs are about 50 yards uphill from where your vehicle is parked. Parking is limited to about four vehicles.

Source map: *Cranbrook Forest District Recreation Map* (BC Forest Service). Phone: 604-426-1700.

120   MIETTE HOT SPRINGS
Jasper National Park Box 10
■   **Jasper, AB T0E 1E0**

A modern, clean, and proper Canadian Parks Service communal plunge in a remote part of beautiful Jasper National Park. Elevation 4,500 feet. Open May to October.

Natural mineral water flows out of several springs at temperatures up to 129° and is piped to two outdoor pools (one of which is wheelchair accessible) ,where it is treated with chlorine and maintained at approximately 104°. Bathing suits are required and can be rented, along with towels, at the facility.

Locker rooms are available on the premises. A cafe, motel, and cabins are available nearby. It is 11 miles to a store, service station, and overnight camping and 15 miles to RV hookups. No credit cards are accepted.

Directions: From the town of Jasper, drive 44 km (26 miles) east on AB 16 to Pocahontas, then turn southeast on Miette Road to the springs.

121A   UPPER HOT SPRING
Banff National Park Box 900
(403) 762-15515
■   **Banff, AB T0L 0C0**

A modern, clean, and proper Parks Canada communal plunge surrounded by the beautiful scenery of Banff National Park, 75 miles west of Calgary. Elevation 5,176 feet. Open all year.

Natural mineral water at 117° flows out of a spring located 50 yards southwest of the pool entrance and is piped to an outdoor swimming pool where it is treated with chlorine. Water temperature in the swimming pool is slightly lower than the current spring output temperature. Bathing suits are required, and suits and towels may be rented at the pool.

Locker rooms are available on the premises. It is one mile to a cafe, store, and motel and four miles to overnight camping and RV hookups. Massage is available by previous arrangement. No credit cards are accepted.

Directions: From the south end of Banff Avenue, follow signs to the spring.

121B   CAVE AND BASIN HOT SPRING
Banff National Park
Banff, AB T0L 0C0

The swimming pool was closed in 1992, and only the interpretive center is currently open.

122 SUNNY CHINOOKS FAMILY NUDIST RECREATIONAL PARK
PO Box 333030   3919 Richmond Rd.
(403) 640-4606
☐   S.W. Calgary, AB T3E 7E2

Rustic and secluded nudist park on 18 acres, 90 minutes from Calgary and one hour from Red Deer. The park is centrally located and close to the Rocky Mountains. Elevation 4,000 feet. Open May through September.

Propane-heated well water is used in a covered hydropool maintained at 102-104° and treated with chlorine. Clothing is always prohibited in the pool and is optional everywhere else on the grounds.

Camping is available on the grounds. The nearest services are 17 miles away in Sundre. No credit cards are accepted.

Note: This is a membership organization not open to the public for drop-in visits, but prospective members may be issued a guest pass by prior arrangement. Telephone or write for information and directions.

With rain a possibility almost all year and some very hot weather in the summer, members appreciate having this gazebo for weather protection.

123 MANITOU SPRINGS MINERAL SPA
PO Box 967   (306) 946-2233
■   Manitou Beach, SK S0K 4T0

Large, new resort hotel and spa featuring indoor pools filled with mineral-rich water pumped from Little Manitou Lake, located 70 miles southeast of Saskatoon. Elevation 500 feet. Open all year.

Lake-bottom mineral springs supply the lake with water three times saltier than the ocean. This highly buoyant water is pumped to three indoor pools, where it is heated with gas and treated with chlorine. The exercise pool is maintained at 94°, the soaking cove is maintained at 98°, and the water massage pool is maintained at 100°. Bathing suits are required.

Hotel rooms, restaurant, bar, gift shop, retail mall, and massage are available on the premises. It is three miles to a service station and a store. Visa and MasterCard are accepted.

Directions: From the town of Watrous, 70 miles southeast of Saskatoon, drive three miles north on SK 365 to Manitou Beach and follow signs to the Spa.

The lake at *Manitou Springs* has a specific density greater than that of the Dead Sea, so it's impossible to sink. What a fun experience!

WASHINGTON

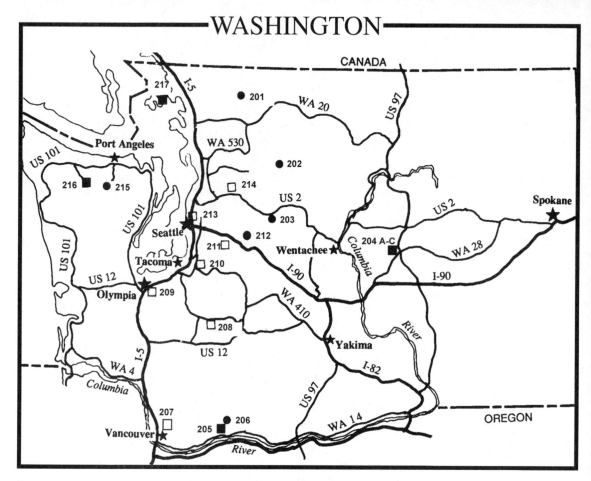

This map was designed to be used with a standard highway map.

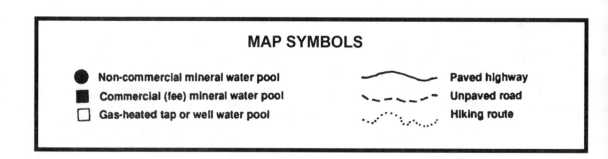

MAP SYMBOLS

● Non-commercial mineral water pool

■ Commercial (fee) mineral water pool

□ Gas-heated tap or well water pool

Paved highway

Unpaved road

Hiking route

201   BAKER HOT SPRINGS

● **North of the town of Concrete**

Charming, primitive spring located at the end of an easy 600-yard path through the lush, green timber of Mt. Baker National Forest. Elevation 2,000 feet. Open all year; winter ski-in or snowmobile.

Natural mineral water bubbles up through vents into the bottom of a large, round, sometimes murky, sandy-bottom pool at 95-100°. Water temperature is controlled by diverting the water from a small, adjacent cold stream. Volcanic ash on the bottom of the pools sometimes clogs vents. Dig down to clear the vents and the water temperature is 102-106°. Water spills out through a channel to a nearby shallow "kiddie pool." The apparent local custom is clothing optional, although there are frequent complaints from users about nudity.

There are no facilities on the premises. There is a private resort and campground located three miles away. Facilities include cabins, camping sites with hookups, boating, and a mini-store. It is 13 miles to a telephone at Lake Tyee Campground. All other services are 20 miles away in Concrete.

Directions: From I-5 at Burlington, five miles north of Mt. Vernon, follow SR 20 approximately 22 miles east to the Baker Lake turnoff. Turn north on Brandy Creek Road for 20 miles to Baker Lake Resort. Directly across from the resort entrance road is a logging road. Follow this unpaved, deeply rutted road for 3.2 miles to a parking turnout on both sides of the road. An unmarked, easy trail begins at the north end of the parking area on your left.

Alternative: From SR 20, follow Baker Lake Road for 18 miles to FR 1130, which is 0.1 miles past the bridge over Boulder Creek. Turn left toward Rainbow Falls. At two miles, where the road forks, continue straight ahead on FR 1130 toward Rainbow Falls. At 1.9 miles, turn right on FR 1141 for .5 miles to the parking turnout. The trail to the springs will be on the right. This is a wider, better graded road than the logging road.

Source map: *Mt. Baker-Snoqualmie National Forest* (hot spring not shown).

Baker Hot Springs

Use unpaved logging road opposite entrance to Baker Lake Resort (other side of Baker Lake Road)

Follow logging road 3.2 miles (clear cut area on right)

Trail to Baker Hot Springs is on left (unmarked)

Follow trail 1/4 mile to hot springs

<u>Use hot springs at your own risk!</u>

So many people ask for directions to the springs that the people at Lake Tyee Campground hand out these cards. However, with only these directions, you might have a rough time finding the springs.

If you are already hiking the Pacific Crest Trail, then a stop at Kennedy Hot Springs to soak would certainly be welcome. Otherwise, you'll have a very long, difficult hike to get to this pool.

● **Southeast of the town of Darrington**

A popular hot spring on a long, five-mile, difficult, uphill trail that eventually connects with the Pacific Crest Trail in the Glacier Peak Wilderness. Elevation 3,300 feet. Open all year.

Natural mineral water flows out of a spring at 96°, directly into a four-foot by five-foot cedar-plank soaking box. A deck surrounds the box, and there is a hanging rail for gear. The rusty-colored water bubbles up vigorously into the bottom of the box at 90-92°. There are no posted clothing requirements.

The only facilities are the pit toilet and a source for drinking water near the cabin. There are undeveloped camp sites near the springs and National Forest campgrounds along Mountain Loop Road. All other services are in Darrington.

Note: Directions and information are available at the Ranger Station. Check for possible avalanche or trail wash-outs with the Darrington Ranger Station: (206) 436-1155. Open daily, May through September; open weekdays only, the rest of the year.

Directions: From I-5, follow SR 530 east for 31 miles to Darrington. From the main intersection turn right and follow SR 20 (Mountain Loop Road) for 10 miles past the junction with road SR 22 to where White Chuck Road (SR 23) comes in on the left (east). Follow this one-lane road 10.3 miles to a large parking area. Trail #643 leads off to the right of the information board at the parking area.

The trail: Trail #634 begins easily, then becomes more strenuous with two series of steep switchbacks. The trail crosses several rivulets and foot-log bridges. When it opens up in a very rocky creekbed, continue straight although the trail seems to disappear. Just past the creekbed, a sign on a tree directs you to Pacific Crest Trail #639 sharply to the left or straight ahead to Kennedy Hot Springs. (Note this sign, it is easy to follow the Pacific Crest Trail by mistake on the way back.)

Continue to a clearing, bearing right toward the river. After crossing a narrow foot-log bridge, take the right fork of the trail, passing signs to a horse camp and pit toilet. Continue a short distance to "Kennedy Cottage." From the cabin, follow the trail to the right. After crossing a bridge over the creek, follow left fork of the trail a few steps to the hot pool.

Source map: *Mt. Baker-Snoqualmie National Forest.*

● **East of the town of Skykomish**

A delightful series of wooden soaking boxes with a spectacular view, located on a steep hillside above the Tyee River in the Mt. Baker-Snoqualmie National Forest. Elevation 3,500 feet. Open all year.

Natural mineral water emerges from several springs at 110° and flows through a hose into the largest of four rectangular, waist-deep soaking tubs lined with plastic. Temperature can be controlled by diverting the inflow hose. A separate cooler source (92°) feeds a smaller, two- to three-person soaking box. Outflow from both tubs flows into lower pools where the temperature becomes progressively cooler. An elaborate series of decks, benches, railing, and stairways connect the pools. The apparent local custom is clothing optional.

There are no services except a pit toilet and amenities (such as plastic bags to pack out your trash) to help keep the place pristine at the spring. National Forest campgrounds are along US 2, and it is 20 miles to all other services in Skykomish.

Directions: Off I-5 from Everett, take US 2 about 50 miles southeast to Skykomish. Continue 10 miles to the tiny town of Scenic. Continue until you see the highway bridge spanning the railroad tracks. Across the bridge on your left is mile marker 59. On your right, watch for a primitive powerline road .2 miles east of of the mile marker. Turn right, and unless you have a four-wheel drive, park as soon as possible and walk up the steep rocky road to a clearing where you see a series of powerlines. From the clearing near tower #7 (look for number plates on the towers), the wide trail S-curves to the southeast. Just past tower #5, on your right, a narrow rocky path arcs uphill through the pines. The trail becomes steeper crossing three seepages on its way to the springs. A heavy gripping rope is tied around trees along two very steep, slippery portions of the trail. Sturdy footgear is recommended.

Note: The springs are on private land within the National Forest. Please respect the property.

Source map: *Mt. Baker-Snoqualmie National Forest* (hot springs not shown on any map).

Natural mineral water is obtained from the city water system through an extra pipe that supplies all of the establishments. Restaurants and all other services are a few blocks away in Soap Lake. Elevation is 1,075 feet, with a dry desert temperate climate and a claim of 300 days of sunshine a year.

This in-room unit has rustic wood walls surrounding a tub for two at *Notaras Lodge*.

204A NOTARAS LODGE
242 Main St. E.   (509) 246-0462
■   **Soap Lake, WA 98851**

Beautiful spruce log lodge with in-room jet tubs and a public bathhouse. Open all year.

Seven of the units are equipped with in-room jet tubs built for two. All rooms have an extra spigot over the bathtub to supply hot mineral water. There is also a bathhouse building containing two private-space, old-fashioned, single bathtubs supplied with mineral water. The bathhouse facilities are available to the public as well as to registered guests.

Massage is available on the premises. Visa and MasterCard are accepted.

204B LAKE MOTEL
322 Daisy S.   (509) 246-1611
■   **Soap Lake, WA 98851**

Large, older downtown motel on main highway.

Twenty-three motel units with double plumbing; kitchenettes available. There is also an outdoor hot tub filled with electrically heated tap water as well as a hot or dry sauna. Visa and MasterCard accepted.

204C THE INN AT SOAP LAKE
226 Main Ave. E.   (509) 246-1132
■   **Soap Lake, WA 98851**

Originally built in 1905 of round river rock. Completely renovated in 1993 with beautifully landscaped grounds and its own private beach right on on Soap Lake. Open all year

A delightful Victorian setting of 20 rooms, a bridal suite, and five cottages. Each room has a freshwater shower and large mineral water soaking tub. Bridal suite has a whirlpool tub.

Kitchenettes, microwaves, and refrigerators are provided. Paddleboats and canoes are available for rent. Fishing, hunting, golfing, and bicycling are available nearby. Major credit cards are accepted.

205 CARSON HOT SPRINGS RESORT
PO Box 370 (509) 427-8292
■ Carson, WA 98610

Picturesque, historic resort that prides itself on having used the same bath methods for over 100 years. Elevation 300 feet. Open all year.

Natural mineral water flows out of a spring at 126° and is piped to men's and women's bathhouses. There are eight claw-footed enamel tubs in the men's bathhouse and nine in the women's. Temperature is controllable in each tub, which is drained and filled after each use, requiring no chemical treatment. An attendant, who is with you at all times, applies a sweat wrap after the soak. Bathing suits are not required in the bathhouses, which are available to the public as well as to registered guests.

Television, radio, and telephones are not available on the premises. Massage, restaurant, hotel rooms, cabins, overnight camping, and RV hookups are available. Reservations are a must. A store and service station are within two miles. Hiking and fishing are nearby. Visa and MasterCard are accepted.

Directions: From the intersection of WA 14 and Bridge of the Gods over the Columbia River, go east on WA 14 and watch for signs. Phone for rates, reservations, and further directions if necessary.

206 ST. MARTINS ON THE WIND
● On Carson H.S. Resort property

Small riverbank soaking pools 100 yards below a waterfall on the Wind River at the end of a sometimes difficult scramble over rocks and boulders. Elevation 150 feet. Open all year. The St. Martin family charges a small fee for use of the pools.

Natural mineral water flows out of several seeps at 107° into shallow, sandy-bottom pools at the river's edge. Moving rocks to admit river water cools the pools. The apparent custom is clothing optional.

There are no services available on the premises, but overnight parking is not prohibited at the parking area. A rustic cabin is available for rent. A restaurant, rooms, and bathhouses are available within one mile at the Carson Hot Springs Resort. It is eight miles to campgrounds in the Gifford Pinchot National Forest and 15 miles to all other services in Hood River.

Directions: As you enter "Home Valley," just east of the Wind River crossing on Hwy 14 (east of Carson), turn left (north) to Berge Road. Drive .8 miles to Indian Cabin Road and turn left. Continue under power pole. Road turns to gravel and dead ends at parking area. A posted sign gives instructions for hiking from there to the springs and for paying the required fee. Sandals and shorts are not recommended as the .5-mile walk is mostly on slippery rocks, and poison oak is abundant.

207   SPA SUITES BY THE HOUR
11819 NE Hwy 99   (206) 573-4815
☐   Vancouver, WA

Tastefully done, rent-a-tub establishment in urban shopping center. Open all year.

Three large rooms (one is handicap-accessible) with chlorine-treated tap water pools heated to 104° or to the customer's request.

Tanning, manicures, stereo, towels and massage are available on the premises. Phone for rates, reservations, and directions.

208   WELLSPRING
Star Route   (206) 569-2514
☐   Ashford, WA 98304

A charming, rustic woodland spa located in a wooded area with a spring-fed pond just outside the southwest entrance to Mt. Rainier National Park. Open all year.

There are two cedar hot tubs, one adjoining pond overlooking a lush forest setting, and one in a private Japanese garden. Each has its own enclosed building with shower and bathroom facilities. Water temperatures are maintained at 104-106° using propane-heated spring water treated with chlorine. Clothing is optional in private spaces.

Facilities include wood-fired cedar saunas and three cozy log cabins. Breakfast basket included with cabin rental. Massage therapy is available on the premises. Visa and MasterCard are accepted. Phone for rates, reservations, and directions.

209   TOWN TUBS AND MASSAGE
115 Olympia Ave. NE (206) 943-2200
☐   Olympia, WA 98501

Modern rent-a-tub establishment in downtown Olympia, two blocks from Percival Landing on Puget Sound.

Private-space hot pools with cedar decks are for rent to the public, using gas-heated tap water treated with chlorine. There are six indoor acrylic pools with the water temperature adjustable from 95-104°. Each unit has a personal sound system.

Therapeutic massage is available on the premises. Visa and MasterCard are accepted. Phone for rates, reservations, and directions.

210   GRAND CENTRAL SAUNA & HOT TUB
32510 Pacific Hwy. So.
    (206) 952-6154
☐   Federal Way, WA 98003

One of a chain of urban locations established by Grand Central, a pioneer in the private rent-a-tub business. Open all year.

Private-space hot pools using chlorine-treated tap water are for rent to the public by the hour. Ten indoor tubs are maintained at temperatures from 102-104°. Each unit contains a sauna.

No credit cards are accepted. Phone for rates, reservations, and directions.

These two scenic tubs at *Wellspring* are as close as you can come to a mineral water soak in semi-wilderness surroundings that are still near the city. One of the best rent-a-pool establishments around.

211   FRATERNITY SNOQUALMIE
PO Box 748   (206) 392-NUDE
☐   Issaquah, WA 98027

Long-established nudist park occupying a hillside fruit orchard surrounded by evergreens, 30 minutes from the Seattle area. Elevation 500 feet. Open to members all year; open to guests from May through September.

The outdoor hydrojet pool is maintained at 104° all year. The outdoor swimming pool is solar heated, ranging from 80° in the summer to 50° in the winter. The wading pool is filled only in the summer. All pools use well water treated with chlorine or bromine. There is also a wood-fired sauna. Clothing is not permitted in pools or sauna.

Two cabins, overnight camping, RV hookups, and a small general store are available on the premises. It is four miles to all other services. Visa and MasterCard are accepted.

Note: This is a membership organization not open to the public for drop-in visits, but prospective members may be issued a guest pass by prior arrangement. Telephone or write for information and directions.

211   GOLDMYER HOT SPRINGS
202 N. 85th St. #106   (206) 789-5631
■   Seattle, WA 98103

Very remote and beautiful mountain hot springs being preserved by a nonprofit volunteer organization. Prior reservations are required, two weeks in advance. Directions are provided with reservations. (A $10 contribution is requested for each adult.) Elevation 1,800 feet. Open all year; high water may make river fording impossible.

Natural mineral water flows into an old horizontal mine shaft at temperatures up to 120°. A dam has been built across the mouth of the shaft, creating a combination steam bath and soaking pool with water temperatures up to 109°. The mineral water also falls into several nearby rock-and-cement soaking pools where the temperature is cooler in each lower pool. No pets, fires, smoking, no alcohol, drugs, glass, weapons, or soap are allowed. Clothing policy is determined by the caretaker based on the wishes of those present.

The 20-mile road to the springs is very rough and the springs are a .5-mile hike from the nearest parking. Overnight camping is available on the premises. It is 28 miles to all other services. Access roads vary in quality from Forest Service Class A to Class D, not suitable for trailers, motor homes and low-clearance vehicles. Ask for a current report on weather and road conditions when phoning for reservations and directions.

You can support the work of this organization by sending tax-deductible contributions to Goldmyer Hot springs/Northwest Wilderness Programs, 202 N. 85th, #106, Seattle, WA 98103.

213　TUBS SEATTLE
4750 Roosevelt Way N.E.

(206) 527-TUBS

☐　Seattle, WA 98105

Large, modern, pool-rental facility located in the University district of Seattle.

Private, luxurious hot pools are for rent to the public, using gas-heated tap water treated with chlorine. There are 12 indoor acrylic spas with water temperature maintained at 102-104°.

Each private suite also includes a dry heat sauna, stereo system, intercom, shower, and modern decor. An 11-bed Sun Salon and a juice bar are also available. TUBS CLUB memberships gain members reservation privileges and discounts. Visa, MasterCard, and American Express are accepted. Phone for rates and directions.

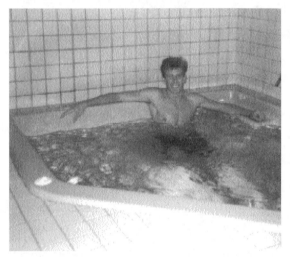

214　LAKE BRONSON CLUB
PO Box 1135　　　(206) 793-0286

☐　Sultan, WA 98294

Beautiful, spacious (320 acres) nudist park with its own 7.5-acre lake, 85-foot waterfall, and evergreen forest. Elevation 600 feet. Open all year.

One large, outdoor hydrojet pool using chlorine-treated artesian well water is maintained at 104°. The spring-fed lake warms to 80° in the summer and freezes over in the winter. There is also an electrically heated sauna. Clothing is prohibited in pool, sauna, and lake and is optional elsewhere.

Rental trailers, laundry facilities, overnight camping, and RV hookups are available on the premises. A cafe is open on weekends and for special events. A teen center, tennis, volleyball, shuffleboard, paddle boats, canoes, and horseshoes are available. It is six miles to all other services. No credit cards are accepted.

Note: This is a membership organization not open to the public for drop-in visits. Interested visitors may be issued a guest pass by prior arrangement. Phone or write for information and directions.

215 OLYMPIC HOT SPRINGS

(see map)

- **South of Port Angeles**

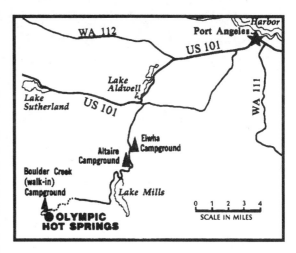

Several user-friendly, primitive springs surrounded by a lush rain forest at the end of a two-mile hike in Olympic National Park. Elevation 1,600 feet. Open all year.

Natural mineral water flows out of several springs at temperatures ranging from 100-112°. Volunteers have built a series of rock-and-sand soaking pools that permit the water to cool down to comfortable soaking temperatures. The hottest pools are those furthest from the creek. Official notices prohibiting nudity are posted often and promptly torn down, resulting in considerable uncertainty. Rangers have been observed issuing a citation only after someone complained and bathers didn't heed orders to dress. However, rangers have not made special trips to the area for the purpose of harassment.

There are no services on the premises, but there is a walk-in campground within 200 yards. It is eight miles to a cafe, store, and service station, seven miles to to Elwha Campground, 5.5 miles to Altaire, and 20 miles to a motel and RV hookups.

Directions: From the city of Port Angeles, go 10 miles west on Olympic Springs Road, turn south and follow signs to Elwha Valley. Paid admission to the National park is required. Continue south 10.3 miles on paved road as it winds up Boulder Creek Canyon to where the road ends. Park and walk the remaining 2.2 miles on the damaged paved road to the old end-of-road parking area. At the west end of that parking area is a quite visible path that brings you to a bridge across Boulder Creek and into the hot-springs area. Most, but not all, paths indicate the presence of a nearby spring.

Conscientious visitors have kept the area litter-free. Please do your part to maintain this standard.

Source map: *NPS Olympic National Park* (hot springs not shown).

Only one of several delightful pools found at the end of a two-mile walk to *Olympic Hot Springs*. Each pool is a different temperature, depending on how far from the river the pool is located.

216　SOL DUC HOT SPRINGS RESORT
　　　PO Box 2169　　　　(206) 327-3583
■　　Port Angeles, WA 98362

Extensively modernized, historic resort surrounded by the evergreen forest of Olympic National Park. Elevation 1,600 feet. Open daily mid-May through September; weekends only in April and October. Pools are for day use only.

Natural mineral water flows out of a spring at 128° and is piped to a heat exchanger, where the spring water heats the shower water and chlorine-treated creek water for the swimming pool. The cooled mineral water is then piped to a large pool, a large soaking pool, and two small pools that are maintained at 74-105° on a flow-through basis, requiring no chemical treatment of the water. These pools are equipped with access ramps for the convenience of disabled persons. All pools are available to the public as well as to registered guests. Bathing suits are required.

Locker rooms, a full-service restaurant, poolside deli bar, gift shop, small grocery store, massage, cabins and RV hookups are available on the premises. It is .25 miles to a National Park campground and 15 miles to a service station. MasterCard, American Express, Discover, and Visa are accepted.

Directions: From US 101, two miles west of Fairholm, take Soleduc River Road 12 miles south to the resort.

This is a picture of the original hotel built in 1912 and modeled after many of the European spas. While the original building is no longer there, you can still enjoy the same waters and the beautiful surroundings of one of the only developed hot springs actually in a national park.

217   DOE BAY VILLAGE RESORT
Orcas Island Star Rt. 86

(206) 376-2291

■   **Olga, WA 98279**

Fantastic combination of running streams, waterfalls, and hot mineral water tubs outdoors on a deck with a spectacular view. Elevation sea level. Open all year.

Natural mineral water is pumped out of a well at 45°, heated by electricity, and piped to two outdoor pools, that are surrounded by trees and adjacent to a running stream with waterfalls. The pool water is continuously filtered, treated with chlorine, and exchanged daily. Each pool is large enough for a dozen people, and one of them has hydrojets. Both are maintained at 101-104°, and a third pool contains cool water at air temperature. The wood-fired sauna is large enough for 20 people. The pools and sauna are available to the public as well as to registered guests. Bathing suits are optional.

Massage, vegetarian meals, general store, rustic cabins, overnight camping, RV hookups, and a hostel-type dormitory are available on the premises. Guided kayak trips and hikes in Moran State Park are nearby. It is 11 miles to a store and service station. All major credit cards are accepted.

Directions: Take the Anacortes Ferry to Orcas Island (about one hour). Go north on Horseshoe Highway for 20.3 miles through Eastsound and Olga to the resort sign for Doe Bay at the east end of island. This very scenic drive takes about one hour.

OREGON

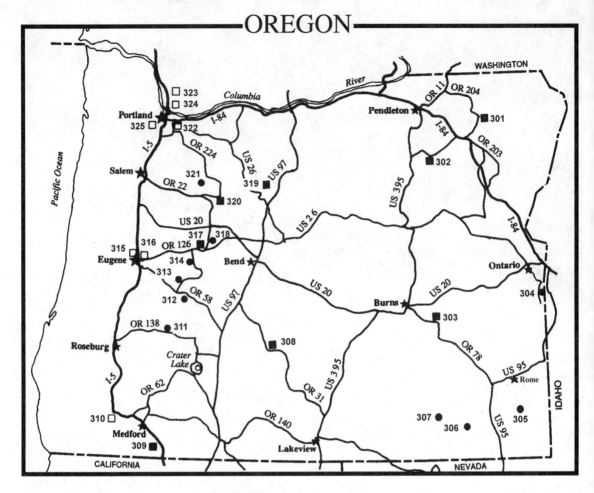

This map was designed to be used with a standard highway

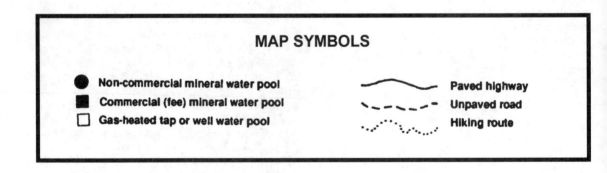

MAP SYMBOLS

● Non-commercial mineral water pool

■ Commercial (fee) mineral water pool

□ Gas-heated tap or well water pool

〰 Paved highway

--- Unpaved road

··· Hiking route

302 LEHMAN HOT SPRINGS
P.O. Box 187   **(503) 427-3015**
■   **Ukiah, OR 97880**

Historic, major hot spring being developed into a large destination resort, surrounded by the beautiful Blue Mountain Forest. Elevation 4,300 feet. Open all year.

Natural mineral water flows out of several springs at temperatures up to 167° and is mixed with cold creek water before being piped to a series of outdoor pools. The first pool ranges from 112-120°, the second pool ranges from 102-110°, and the swimming pool ranges from 85-90° in the summer and from 90-96° in the winter. All pools operate on a flow-through basis. The pools are available to the public as well as to registered guests. Bathing suits are required.

Lodging (log cabins, tepees), dressing rooms, mineral water showers, snack bar, game room, RV hookups, camping, and hiking trails are available on the premises. Horses, hay rides, hunting safaris, fishing, cross country skiing, mountain biking, and snowmobiling are available nearby. A store, service station, and motel are located 18 miles away in Ukiah. Visa and MasterCard are accepted.

Future development plans call for more cabins, a small shopping center, hotel/restaurant, home sites ,and a nine-hole golf course. Phone for status of construction.

Directions: From La Grande, drive eight miles west on I-84 to OR 244, then west for 35 miles. Watch for Lehman Hot Springs signs. From Ukiah, take OR 244 18 miles east to the hot springs exit.

301 COVE SWIMMING POOL
907 Water St.   **(503) 568-4890**
■   **Cove, OR 97824**

Large swimming pool and picnic grounds in the foothills of the Wallowa Mountains. Elevation 3,200 feet. Open May 1 through Labor Day.

Natural mineral water at 86° flows up from a hot spring in the gravel bottom of the pool. Thanks to this continual flow-through, no chlorine is added. Bathing suits are required.

Picnic grounds and snack bar are available on the premises. It is two blocks to a cafe, store, and service station and 15 miles to a motel. No credit cards are accepted.

Directions: From I-84 in La Grande, take OR 82 exit and go east to OR 237, then 14 miles south to the town of Cove.

303   CRYSTAL CRANE HOT SPRINGS
HC 53-2653 Hwy 78   (503) 493-2312
■   Burns, OR 97720

A growing, 340-acre health-oriented resort in the wide-open spaces of the eastern Oregon high desert. Cranes, avocets, and other birds often visit the pond. Elevation 4,200 feet. Open all year.

Natural mineral water flows out of several springs at 185° and supplies six private-space tubs where hot and cold mineral water valves are controlled by the customer to obtain the desired temperature. The mineral water also fills a large, 80-foot pond where temperatures range from 95-105°. All the pools operate on a flow-through basis so that no chemical treatment of the water is necessary. Most facilities are handicap accessible. Bathing suits are not required in the private-space pools.

Facilities include cabins, an organic greenhouse, and a camping area. A small snack bar and microwave are available. Massage and vegetarian drinks are available on the premises. It is four miles to the nearest store and 24 miles to all other services in Burns. No credit cards are accepted.

Future plans include overnight facilities, RV hookups, a convention hall, and a vegetarian restaurant. A nine-unit motel is under construction. Call for status of construction.

Directions: From Burns, drive 24.5 miles east on OR 78 and watch for signs.

An organic greenhouse makes a great start for this growing health-oriented resort. The setting already offers wide-open spaces and a wonderful large, warm pond—plus indoor soaking tubs supplied by several springs that provide an abundance of hot water.

● **Southwest of the town of Owyhee**

Easily accessible, primitive hot spring on the river's edge in the Owyhee River canyon. Elevation 2,400 feet. Open all year.

Natural mineral water flows out of several springs and a concrete standpipe at temperatures of more than 150° and then flows toward the river where volunteers have built several rock-and-sand soaking pools. The temperature in the pools is controlled by varying the amount of cold river water permitted to enter. The pools are visible from the road, so bathing suits are advisable although the common consent of those present seems to prevail.

There are no services available on the premises except for a large parking area where overnight parking is not prohibited. It is 10 miles to a cafe, store, and service station and 18 miles to a motel and RV hookups.

Directions: From the town of Owyhee, on OR 201, follow signs west toward Owyhee Lake and State Park. When the road enters Owyhee Canyon look for a large, metal water pipe running up a steep slope on the west side of the road. Go 1.4 miles beyond that metal pipe and look on the river side of the road for a large stone and cement outhouse, a low concrete standpipe from which steaming water is flowing, and a large dirt parking area.

Source map: USGS *Owyhee Dam, Oregon.*

The federal lands around *Snively* are administered by the Bureau of Land Management and have been designated a "watchable wildlife area." The canyon is home to a wide variety of frogs, reptiles, deer, bobcats, river otters, beaver, weasels, and multiple species of birds, including eagles, hawks, owls, herons, egrets, and ducks.

The rope hanging over the rocks is a clue to the hikers that behind those boulders is a beautiful pool and waterfall just waiting for them after this steep scramble up from the river.

● **Southeast of the city of Rome**

Two small pools on the east side of the river and a gem of a secluded pool and waterfall on the other. Located in the upper Owyhee River Canyon, south of Jordan Valley, with spectacular sunsets visible from springs and nearby campground. Elevation 4,000 feet. Open all year; wet weather may make roads impassable, and high water makes it dangerous to ford the river.

Natural mineral water flows at 95° from several sets of springs on the east bank and winds its way through the grass toward the river and into two small pools. On the west bank, several showers cascade 95° water into a beautifully clear, gravel-bottom pool. The prevailing custom is clothing optional.

It is three miles to Three Forks, a primitive BLM campground, and 51 miles to all other services in Rome.

Directions: From Rome, proceed 18.2 miles east on OR 95 to milepost 36. Turn right on excellent gravel road (sign says 36 miles to Three Forks). Thirty miles later you are on a bluff looking down at a campground. Take this very rough, switchback road two miles downhill to campground. Trailers and motorhomes not recommended. High clearance, four-wheel drive vehicles are best. At bottom of hill, turn right for campground and left for spring.

To reach the spring on east the side, cross wooden bridge, open (and close) barbed wire gate, and proceed 2.2 miles over very rough, rocky road to spring. When you reach the high bluff, get out and look down at the springs. You may want to park here and walk the remaining distance as the short road from the bluff down to springs is steep and rough.

To reach the waterfall on the west side cross the river only during low water and look for waterfall. Climb up a short distance to the pool among the rocks.

Note: The springs are on private, unposted land. Please take particular care to leave nothing but footprints.

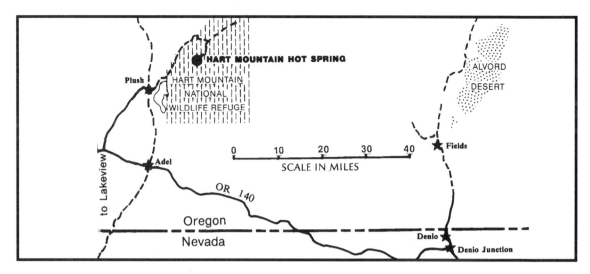

306 WHITEHORSE RANCH HOT SPRING

● **Southeast of Burns Junction**

A very remote, primitive hot spring requiring about 26 miles of unpaved road travel in the dry, southeastern corner of Oregon in the Alvord Desert. Elevation 4,000 feet. Open all year.

Natural mineral water flows out of a spring at 114° and into a small, volunteer-built soaking pool that ranges in temperature from 104-112°. The overflow runs into a larger second pool that ranges in temperature from 70-90°, depending on air temperature and wind conditions. The apparent local custom is clothing optional.

There are no services on the premises, but there is plenty of level space on which overnight parking or tenting is not prohibited, and there is a new concrete outhouse. It is 45 miles to all services in Burns Junction.

Directions: From Burns Junction on US 95, go 21 miles south on US 95, then turn west on a gravel road and go 21 miles to Whitehorse Ranch. About 2.5 miles past the ranch, where the fence line ends, turn left on well-traveled dirt road. Drive 2.5 miles to the spring. If you miss this road, proceed approximately five miles from the ranch and turn left on a dirt road. Immediately take the left fork. Utility pole on right is B 281. Drive 2.1 miles. Bear right at old cattle loading ramp. Spring is on right, and a new concrete toilet is just past the spring on left.

Source map: BLM *Southern Malheur*.

307 HART MOUNTAIN HOT SPRING
(see map)

● **North of the town of Adel**

Semi-improved hot spring enclosed by a roofless, cement block wall and surrounded by miles of barren plateau within the Hart Mountain National Antelope Refuge. Elevation 6,000 feet. Open all year.

Natural mineral water flows out of a spring at 98°. The edge of the spring has been cemented to create a soaking pool that maintains that temperature. There is no posted clothing policy, which leaves it up to the mutual consent of those present.

There are no services available on the premises, but there is an abundance of level ground on which overnight parking is not prohibited. It is 20 miles to a cafe and store and 40 miles to all other services.

Source map: *Hart Mountain National Antelope Refuge*.

308   SUMMER LAKE HOT SPRINGS
(503) 943-3931

■   **Paisley, OR 97636**

Small, indoor plunge in the wide-open spaces south of Summer Lake. Elevation 4,200 feet. Open all year.

Natural mineral water flows out of a spring at 118° and cools as it is piped to the pool building. Water temperature in the indoor pool is maintained at 102° in the winter and 100° in the summer on a continuous flow-through basis that requires no chemical treatment of the water. Bathing suits are required.

Dressing rooms, overnight camping, and RV hookups are available on the premises. It is six miles to all other services. No credit cards are accepted.

Location: Six miles northwest of the town of Paisley on OR 31. Watch for sign on north side of road.

309   JACKSON HOT SPRINGS
2253 Hwy 99 N.   (503) 482-3776
■   **Ashland, OR 97520**

Historic resort with public plunge, indoor soaking tubs, picnic grounds, and RV park. Elevation 1,650 feet. Open all year. Swimming pool open May 1 to October 31.

Natural mineral water flows out of three springs at 100-115° and directly into an outdoor swimming pool that is treated with chlorine and maintains a temperature of 84-90°. There are three indoor individual soaking tubs large enough for two persons each, in which heated natural mineral water can be controlled up to 110°. These tubs are drained and cleaned after each use so that no chemical treatment of the water is necessary. Bathing suits are required, except in private rooms.

Dressing rooms, picnic grounds, cabins, overnight camping, RV hookups, and a cafe are available on the premises. There is a store and service station within two blocks. Visa and MasterCard are accepted.

Location: Two miles north of Ashland at the Valley View Road exit from US 99.

310   CEDAR CREST HOT TUB RENTALS
227 N.E. Hillcrest Drive   (503) 474-3090
☐   Grants Pass, OR 97526

Clean and spacious rent-a-tub establishment located in north Grants Pass, near the K-Mart plaza.

Four fiberglass tubs using gas-heated, chlorine-treated tap water are for rent to the public by the hour. Water temperature in the tubs varies from 100°-104°. No credit cards are accepted.

Phone for rates, reservations, and directions.

---

311   UMPQUA WARM SPRING
(see map)

●   **Northwest of Crater Lake**

Popular, small, semi-improved hot spring on a wooded bluff overlooking North Umpqua River. Located in the Umpqua National Forest at the end of a short path. Elevation 2,600 feet. Open all year.

Natural mineral water flows out of a spring at 108° and directly into a sheltered, six-foot by six-foot pool that volunteers have carved out of the spring-built travertine deposit. There are no posted clothing requirements, and the location is quite remote, so a clothing-optional custom would be expected. However, the location is so popular, especially on summer weekends, that it is advisable to take a bathing suit with you. You may have to wait your turn to share a rather crowded pool.

There are no services available on the premises. It is three miles to a Forest Service campground and 25 miles to all other services.

Directions: Drive 60 miles east of Roseburg on OR 138 to Toketee Junction. Turn north on paved road FS 34 (Toketee Rigdon Road). Drive 2.3 miles, turn right on FS 3401 (Thorn Prairie Road), and drive two miles to the parking area. Walk across the bridge over the North Umpqua River, bear right on the North Umpqua Trail, and climb .25 miles east to springs.

Source map: *Umpqua National Forest.*

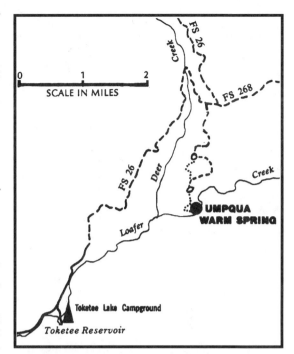

The pool inside the shelter is often very crowded both during the summer and on the weekends. Bring your lunch and wait your turn. Also bring mosquito repellent in the summer.

67 OREGON

312   MCCREDIE HOT SPRINGS

● **East of the town of Oakridge**

Easily accessible, primitive hot springs with a strong skinny-dipping tradition, located on the north and south banks of Salt Creek in the Willamette National Forest. Elevation 2,100 feet. Open all year for day use only.

Natural mineral water flows out of several springs on the north bank at 120° and on the south bank at 140°. The water is channeled into a series of shallow, volunteer-built, rock-and-mud pools where it cools as it flows toward the creek. The pools on the south bank tend to be larger and around 100°. There are hot jets on the bottom of the creek, so be careful. Despite the proximity of a main highway, the apparent local custom is clothing optional.

There are no services available on the premises. There is a large, level area nearby in which parking is permitted from sunrise to sunset only. It is less than one mile to a Forest Service campground and 10 miles to all other services.

Directions: To reach the springs and pools on the north bank drive from the town of Oakridge, drive drive approximately 10 miles east on OR 58 past Blue Pool Campground. At .1 miles past mile marker 45, turn right (south) into a large parking area between the road and the creek. Walk to the upstream (east) end of the parking area and follow a well-worn path 40 yards to the springs.

This less-crowded, idyllic soak on the south bank of Salt Creek is also part of the popular *McCredie Hot Springs'* series of pools.

To reach the springs and soaking pools on the south bank, drive .5 miles east on OR 58, turn right on Shady Gap Road across the bridge, and stay right on FS 5875. Drive .1 miles, park, and look for an overgrown path that follows the creek .25 miles back downstream to the pools.

These shallow pools on the north bank are fed by some very hot water, but thanks to the river, there is plenty of available cool water to enjoy a soak, a talk, or a special warm mud massage. Even though McCredie Hot Springs is right off the road and very popular, a relaxed attitude prevails and there is room for all.

Warm water and cool mornings produce this mystical hot-springs soak pictured on the left.

Whether you go alone or with friends, this pool provides a delicious warm soak amid ferns and trees, and it is only a short distance from the trail.

313   MEDITATION POOL (WALL CREEK) WARM SPRING
● **Northeast of the town of Oakridge**

Idyllic, primitive warm spring on the wooded banks of Wall Creek at the end of a short, easy trail in the Willamette National Forest. Elevation 2,200 feet. Open all year for day use only.

Natural mineral water flows up through the gravel bottom of a volunteer-built, rock-and-sand pool at 104°. The pool temperature ranges up to 96° depending on air temperature and wind conditions. While the water is not hot enough for therapy soaking, it is ideal for effortless lolling. The apparent local custom is clothing optional.

There are no services available on the premises. It is five miles from the trailhead to a Forest Service campground and nine miles to all other services.

Directions: On OR 58 in the town of Oakridge at the "city center" highway sign, turn north on Rose Street over the train tracks. At First Street, turn east and keep going as that street becomes FS 24. Nine miles from firehouse, turn (left) north on FS 1934 (sign says "Blair Lake 8 miles') for .5 miles on gravel road and watch for trailhead sign on (left) west side of the road. There is no name or number given for the trail at the trailhead area. Follow a well-worn path along Wall Creek for 600 yards to the creekside pool. Tree sign says "Warm Springs Trail.")

Source map: *Willamette National Forest*.

314 TERWILLIGER (COUGAR) HOT SPRINGS

(see map)

● **Southeast of the town of Blue River**

A lovely series of user-friendly, log-and-stone soaking pools in a picturesque, forest canyon at the end of an easy .25-mile trail in the Willamette National Forest. Elevation 3,000 feet. Open all year for day use only.

Natural mineral water flows out of a spring at 116° and directly into the first of a series of volunteer-built pools, each of which is a few degrees cooler than the one above. Water temperature may vary depending on flow. An organized group of volunteers has also built access steps and railings. The apparent local custom is clothing optional.

There are no services available on the premises. There is a walk-in campground within .5 miles. Overnight parking is prohibited along the road for one mile on both sides of the trailhead. It is four miles to a Forest Service campground and eight miles to all other services.

Directions: From OR 126 approximately five miles east of Blue River, turn south on FS 19 along the west side of Cougar Reservoir. The marked hot-springs trailhead is on the west side of the road just past milepost 7 and .3 miles south of Boone Creek. A large parking area is on the east side of the road, .1 miles beyond the trailhead. Parking is permitted from sunrise to sunset only.

Reference map: *Willamette National Forest* (hot springs not shown).

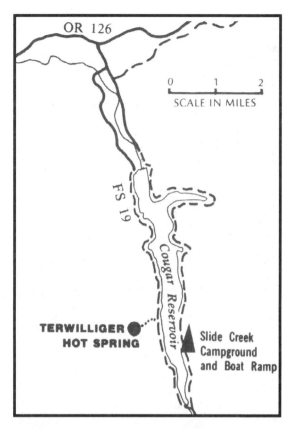

315   SPRINGFIELD SPAS
        1100 Main St.   (503) 741-1777
☐   Springfield, OR 97477

Well-maintained, suburban, rent-a-tub establishment located on the main street in downtown Springfield.

Private-space hydrojet pools using chlorine-treated tap water are for rent to the public by the hour. Twelve fiberglass tubs in open-roof enclosed spaces are maintained at 102°. Each unit includes a covered dressing area with shower and stereo.

Three tanning beds are available on the premises. Visa, MasterCard and Discover are accepted. Phone for rates, reservations, and directions.

316   ONSEN HOT TUB RENTALS
        1883 Garden Ave.   (503) 345-9048
☐   Eugene, OR 97403

Well-maintained, enclosed, rent-a-tub establishment located near the University of Oregon.

Private-space hydrojet pools using chlorine-treated tap water are for rent to the public by the hour. Fourteen fiberglass tubs in open-roof enclosed spaces are maintained at 102°. Each unit includes a covered dressing area.

No credit cards are accepted. Phone for rates, reservations, and directions.

317 BELKNAP LODGE AND HOT SPRINGS
P.O. Box 1   (503) 822-3512
■ **Belknap Springs, OR 97413**

Attractive, riverside resort in a wilderness setting with in-room jet tubs, campground, and RV park, surrounded by the lush greenery of Willamette National Forest. Elevation 1,700 feet. Open all year.

Natural mineral water flows out of a spring at 196° and is piped into a combination reservoir and heat exchanger where heat is extracted for space heating and for the hot water supply in the lodge and the RV park. The cooled mineral water is piped to outdoor pools at the lodge and the RV park. Both pools are lightly treated with chlorine and maintained at a temperature of 100-102° in the winter and 100° in the summer. Four lodge rooms have indoor hydrojet tubs controllable up to 110°. These tubs are drained and cleaned after each use so that no chemical treatment of the water is needed. The pools are available to the public as well as to registered guests. Bathing suits are required, except in private rooms.

Rooms, overnight camping, RV hookups, massage, a general store, fishing, and white water rafting are available on the premises. Suits and towels are for rent. It is six miles to all other services. Visa and MasterCard are accepted.

Location: On OR 126, six miles east of the town of McKenzie Bridge. Follow signs.

318 BIGELOW HOT SPRING

● **Northeast of the town of McKenzie Bridge**

A small, rock-and-sand pool in a fern-lined grotto on the McKenzie River. Elevation 2,000 feet. Open all year.

A small flow of natural mineral water (130°) bubbles up from the bottom of a volunteer-dug pool, maintaining a comfortable 102-104° soaking temperature. The apparent local custom is clothing optional.

There are no services available on the premises. It is 1.5 miles to a campground (Ollalie), three miles to a motel and RV hookups (Belknap Hot Springs), and six miles to all other services.

Directions: From the town of McKenzie Bridge, drive nine miles northeast on OR 126. Drive .4 miles past milepost 15, then turn left onto FS 2654 (Deer Creek Road). Park just beyond the bridge over the McKenzie River. Follow the signed McKenzie River Trail a short way south and watch for the second faint path heading down the steep bank to the pool at the river's edge.

A little rain didn't discourage this family from soaking; they simply moved back into the grotto.

319 KAH-NEE-TA VACATION RESORT VILLAGE

PO Box K   (503) 553-1112
■ **Warm Springs, OR 97761**

A modern resort owned and operated by the Confederated Tribes of the Warm Springs Indian Reservation. In these foothills on the east side of the Cascade Mountains, the sun shines 300 days a year. Elevation 1,500 feet. Open all year.

Natural mineral water flows out of a spring at 140° and is piped to the bathhouse and swimming pool. The large outdoor swimming pool is chlorinated and maintained at a temperature of 95°. The men's and women's bathhouses each contain five tiled Roman tubs in which the soaking temperature is individually controlled up to 110°. Tubs are drained and filled after each use. Pools and bathhouses are available to the public as well as to registered guests. Bathing suits are required in public areas.

Massage, dressing rooms, restaurant, cabins, tepees, overnight camping, RV hookups, and miniature golf are available on the premises. A resort hotel, golf course, and convention facilities for up to 750 people are also located on the property. It is 11 miles to a store and service station. Visa, MasterCard, American Express, Diners Club, and Carte Blanche are accepted.

Directions: From US 26 in Warm Springs, follow signs 11 miles northeast to resort.

Close to both private and commercial airstrips, this fully equipped resort can provide space for a huge convention or offer a night's stay in a tepee. The focal point of the 600,000-acre reservation is the Museum at Warm Springs —Oregon's first Native American museum.

320   BREITENBUSH HOT SPRINGS RETREAT AND CONFERENCE CENTER
■ PO Box 578   (503) 854-3314
   Detroit, OR 97342

A rustic, older resort that has been renovated by the intentional community that operates the retreat center as a worker-owned cooperative. The resort is located on the banks of the Breitenbush River, surrounded by the Willamette National Forest. Elevation 2,300 feet. Open all year.

Natural mineral water flows out of springs and artesian wells at temperatures up to 180°. There are four outdoor soaking pools using flow-through mineral water requiring no chemical treatment. Each pool is maintained at a different temperature that ranges from 60-111°. There are three outdoor pools in the meadow that operate on a flow-through basis with temperatures averaging between 100-110°, depending on weather conditions. The sauna/steambath building is supplied with 180° water direct from an adjoining well and spring. The pools are available to the public for day use as well as to overnight guests, but prior reservations are strongly advised. Clothing is optional in the tubs and sauna area unless a workshop leader requests special swimsuit-required times.

Massage, hydrotherapy, aromatherapy, and spiritual counseling (by reservation), as well as vegetarian meals, and cabins are available on the premises. Daily well-being programs are offered without charge.

It is 11 miles to a store, service station and phone, 1.5 miles to overnight camping and 70 miles to RV hookups. Organizations and individuals are invited to request rates for facilities suitable for seminars and conferences. Visa and MasterCard are accepted.

Location: Eleven miles northeast of Detroit. Phone for rates, reservations, and directions.

Whether you are attending a spiritual seminar or are on a mushroom hunt, *Breitenbush Hot Springs* with its access to the river— and several tubs to view it from— makes an ideal place to relax and enjoy nature.

77   OREGON

(see map)

● **Southeast of the town of Estacada**

One of the best: a well-planned rustic facility featuring hot mineral water supplied through a 150-foot log flume. A lush rain forest and tumbling mountain stream make the 1.5 mile access trail enjoyable in its own right. Elevation 2,200 feet. Open all year.

Natural mineral water emerges from two springs at 135° and is flumed to an outdoor, round cedar tub on a deck at the upper spring site and to two bathhouse buildings at the lower spring site. The partially-roofed bathhouse is a replica of the one that burned down in 1979 and offers five hand-hewn cedar tubs in private rooms. The open-sided bathhouse offers a single communal space containing three hewn tubs and a round cedar tub. A flume diversion gate at each tub brings in more hot water whenever desired, and all tubs are drained and cleaned daily so that no chemical treatment of the water is necessary. There are no posted clothing requirements, and the apparent local custom in the communal bathhouse is clothing optional.

All facilities are made possible and are managed by the Friends of Bagby Hot Springs, Inc., a non-profit volunteer organization operating under a special use permit with the Forest Service to restore, preserve, and maintain the area. Volunteers also serve as hosts for the public. You can support this pioneering organization by sending tax-deductible contributions to Friends of Bagby, Inc., PO Box 15116, Portland, OR 97215.

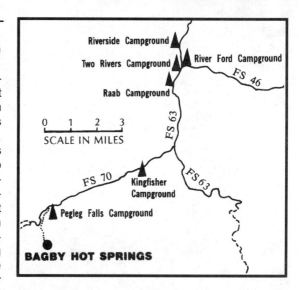

There is a picnic area on the premises, but no overnight camping is permitted. A walk-in campground is located at Shower Creek, .33 miles down the trail beyond Bagby. A drive-in Forest Service Campground (Nohorn) is located adjacent to the trailhead parking area, and the Pegleg Falls Campground is located .5 miles northeast of the trailhead. All other services are available 32 miles away in Estacada.

This sign is posted at the trailhead into the springs.

A network of wood flumes and pipes carries the hot water to the individually controlled tubs in the bathhouse—a replica of the one that burned down in the 1970s. The half roof seems to be slanted in such a way as to keep the sun off in summer and the snow away in winter. The walk in through an absolutely gorgeous forest and along fern-lined streams only adds to the anticipated pleasure of a delightful soak.

322   FOUR SEASONS HOT TUBBING
19059 S.E. Division   (503) 666-3411
☐   Gresham, OR 97030

Attractive, suburban rent-a-tub facility featuring enclosed outdoor tubs. Open all year.

Private-space hot pools using chlorine-treated tap water are for rent to the public by the hour. Six enclosed, outdoor fiberglass hydrojet pools are maintained at a temperature of 104°. Each unit includes indoor dressing room, shower, and toilet. Visa and MasterCard are accepted. Phone for rates, reservations, and directions.

323   OPEN AIR HOT TUBBING
11126 N.E. Halsey   (503) 257-8191
☐   Portland, OR 97220

Unique, suburban rent-a-tub featuring open-roofed wood patios. Open all year.

Private-space hot pools using chlorine-treated tap water are for rent to the public by the hour. Six enclosed, outdoor fiberglass hydrojet pools are maintained at temperatures ranging from 102-104°. Each unit has an outdoor water spray over the pool and an indoor dressing room with shower and toilet. Three of the units can be combined to accommodate a party of 24. There is a sauna in one unit. The apparent local custom is clothing optional.

AM/FM cassettes, cable television, VCR in two rooms, and a sauna are available for use. An open-air tanning salon is also on the premises. Visa and MasterCard are accepted. Phone for rates, reservations, and directions.

Inner City Hot Springs attempts to provide a full repertoire of classes and services for people who are into relaxation, healing, and growth.

324   INNER CITY HOT SPRINGS, COMMON
        GROUND WELLNESS CENTER
        2927 N.E. Everett   (503) 238-0244
☐   Portland, OR 97232

Open-air, family-style pools and sauna in a garden setting near downtown Portland.

Two communal hydrojet pools, cold pool, flotation tanks, sauna, and sun deck are for rent to the public by the hour. Both hot pools use gas-heated tap water treated with chlorine and are maintained at 104°. Bathing suits are optional in the pool and sauna areas.

Hakomi therapy, yoga, massage, child care, homeopathy, rebirthing, and acupressure are available on the premises. No credit cards are accepted. Phone for rates, reservations, and directions.

325   ELITE TUBBING AND TANNING
        4240 S.W. 10th   (503) 641-7727
☐   Beaverton, OR 97005

Private rent-a-tub suites in a remodeled house across from Beaverton's Montgomery Ward store. Open all year.

Private-space hot pools using chlorine-treated tap water are for rent to the public by the hour. Six indoor fiberglass hydrojet pools are maintained at a temperature of 103°. Each suite includes a shower and toilet.

Facilities include tanning equipment. Massage is available on the premises. Visa and MasterCard are accepted. Phone for rates, reservations, and directions.

IDAHO

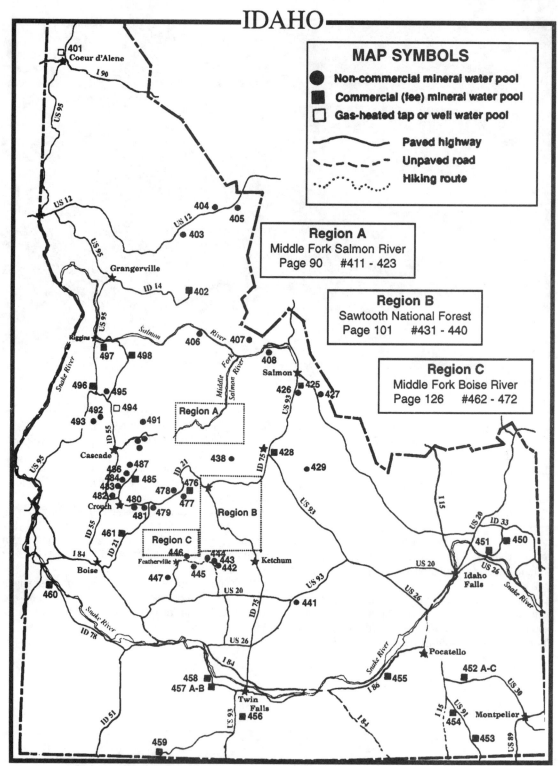

MAP SYMBOLS

● Non-commercial mineral water pool
■ Commercial (fee) mineral water pool
□ Gas-heated tap or well water pool

～～～ Paved highway
– – – Unpaved road
··········· Hiking route

Region A
Middle Fork Salmon River
Page 90   #411 - 423

Region B
Sawtooth National Forest
Page 101   #431 - 440

Region C
Middle Fork Boise River
Page 126   #462 - 472

This map was designed to be used with a standard highway map.

An aquarium and fish nets are ideal decor for a motel located on a lake noted for its fishing and where the American bald eagle dives for Salmon.

401 BENNETT BAY INN
E 5144 I-90   (208) 664-6168
☐   Coeur D'Alene, ID 83814

Rustic older motel with hot pool theme suites, overlooking Lake Coeur d'Alene, referred to by *National Geographic* as one of the five most beautiful lakes in the world. Located 3.5 miles from downtown Coeur d'Alene and 30 miles east of Spokane, Washington, along a road that was the major highway before I-90 was built.

Seven of the 21 rooms are themed hot-tub rooms with motifs such as Fantasy Room, Hawaiian Room, Montana Room, which is a four-room suite, etc. The fiberglass tubs use well water that is pumped in by electricity on a continuous flow-through basis, treated with chlorine and heated to 102°. Additional theme rooms are being revamped by the owners.

Facilities include refrigerator, microwave, and storage in each room. All but four rooms face the lake. There is also a large deck with picnic tables and a lakeside view. Visa, MasterCard, American Express, and Diners Club are accepted. Phone for rates, reservations, and directions.

402 RED RIVER HOT SPRINGS
                        (208) 983-2000
■   Elk City, ID 83525

Friendly, remote, rustic resort featuring both public and private-space pools surrounded by the tall timber in the Nez Perce National Forest. Elevation 4,500 feet. Open all year.

Natural mineral water flows out of 10 springs at temperatures up to 130°. The chlorine-treated swimming pool water varies from 88° in the summer to 72° in the winter. The outdoor flow-through soaking pool is maintained at 104° and requires no chemical treatment. There are also three, claw-footed bathtubs located in private spaces. These are drained and cleaned after each use. In a fourth private space, there is an authentic galvanized horse trough that is surprisingly comfortable for a two-person soak. Pools are available to the public as well as to registered guests. Bathing suits are required in public areas.

Locker rooms, a cafe, store, rustic cabins, and overnight camping are available on the premises. Hiking, fishing, cross-country skiing, snowmobiling, and horse trails are nearby. It is 30 miles to a service station and 150 miles to RV hookups. No credit cards are accepted.

Directions: From the town of Grangeville, take ID 14 to Elk City, then go 25 miles east to the resort. The last 11 miles are on an easy gravel road.

Red River Hot Springs found the perfect way to recycle a horse trough, and it does make a very comfortable place for two people to soak.

Directions: On US 12, drive 25 miles northeast of Lowell to the Lochsa Historical Ranger Station and Visitors Center. One mile past is the turnoff for Wilderness Gateway Campground. Go past Loops A and B and the amphitheater. Just before crossing a bridge, notice trailhead sign for Trail 211 on the left. Cross the bridge to trail parking area. Follow Trail 211 for five miles in a continuous ascent. The first half-mile is sharp,steep switchbacks. During summer months it is best to set out early in the day when most of the trail is still shaded. Five miles up when the trail forks, hikers need to follow Trail 221 to the right, descending half a mile to a flat campsite area. Cross the ingenious double-foot log bridge. When the trail forks after the bridge, turn left. This trail gently ascends for a 10- to 15-minute walk until it curves around to the right, to a large open area where the pools are located.

You may pass pack teams of horses, burros, etc. An outfitter is available near the trailhead.

Source maps: USGS *Huckleberry Butte*; *Clearwater National Forest*.

403   STANLEY HOT SPRINGS

● **Northeast of the town of Lowell**

A series of delightful rock and log soaking pools in Huckleberry Creek canyon at the end of a rugged five-mile trail in the Selway-Bitterroot Wilderness. Elevation 3,600 feet. Open all year.

Natural mineral water flows out of a canyon bank at 115° and cools as it tumbles through a series of volunteer-built, log-and-rock pools that range in temperature from 90-110°. The cold creek flowing alongside offers a refreshing place to cool off. The apparent local custom is clothing optional.

There are no services available on the premises, but there are spacious campsites for backpackers and pack teams tucked into the nearby woods, where camping is permitted for up to 14 days. There is a drive-in Forest Service fee campground at the trailhead. All other services are in Lowell, 26 miles west from the trailhead, or at Powell Junction, 39 miles east.

Stanley Hot Springs is one of the delightful hot springs possibly visited by Lewis and Clark when they traversed one of the most difficult passages through the Bitterroot Mountains and across the Continental Divide. While the Nez Perce Indians helped the explorers as much as they could, this double-footed bridge was not there to help the travelers cross the river.

404   WEIR CREEK HOT SPRINGS

●   **Northeast of the town of Lowell**

Secluded, primitive hot springs and creekside soaking pool reached via a sometimes difficult rocky half-mile path in Clearwater National Forest. Elevation 2,900 feet. Open all year.

Natural mineral water flows out of several springs at 117° and down the side of the mountain where it is channeled through a wooden gutter to a large volunteer-built, eight-to-ten person, rock-bottomed pool lined with split logs. Temperature can be controlled by moving the gutter to add or divert the flow of hot water. Wooden plank benches frame the pool on three sides.

Water flows into an adjoining rock-bottomed pool at 100°. Continual flow-through keeps water in both pools fresh. From the bottom of the large pool a metal pipe carries water to a one-person pool below where it showers out at 95°. It is a short but steep, slippery, muddy walk down to this little pool just a few feet below. Fifty feet farther uphill, a small slimy-bottomed three-person rock pool has been built by volunteers over a water seepage where pool temperature is 100°. There is no flow-through and the water appears murky. The apparent local custom is clothing optional, although on a busy summer day you many encounter many families wearing swimwear.

There are no services available on the premises. It is eight miles to a Forest Service campground and 20 miles to all other services at Powell junction. Along the creek there are a few level pack-in campsites with fire pits.

Directions: From Lowell, drive 45 miles northeast on US 12 to mile marker 142. Just .1 miles past on the left, is a deep pullout on the inland side of highway, around a big curve and easy to miss. Coming from the east on US 12 from Powell, watch for mile marker 143, where a wooden bridge crosses the Lochsa River at the trailhead for Mocus Point. Go .9 miles past the bridge, look for the deep turnout on the inland side to the road. There are no signs indicating Weir Creek, only signs reminding visitors to pack out all trash, which they seem to do.

Follow the unmarked, unmaintained path on the west side of the creek for slightly less than .5 miles, staying close to the creek and not taking any spur trails heading uphill to the left. The trail climbs over rocks, fallen trees and one large boulder creekside where it seems to disappear, but it resumes on the other side of the boulder. There are muddy spots where hot water seeps up from underground, and some rock hopping is required along the creek. A series of primitive steps leads uphill to the left to the soaking pools.

Source map: *Clearwater National Forest.*

405　JERRY JOHNSON HOT SPRINGS
(see map)

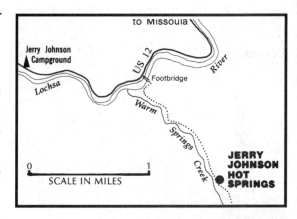

● **Southwest of the town of Missoula**

Delightful group of user-friendly, primitive hot springs at the end of an easy, one-mile hike through a beautiful forest along the east bank of Warm Springs Creek. Elevation 3,200 feet. Open all year for day use only.

Odorless natural mineral water flows out of many fissures in the creek bank at 114° and also out of several other springs at temperatures up to 110°. Volunteers have constructed rock-and-mud soaking pools along the edge of the river and near the springs. The temperature within each pool is controlled by admitting cold creek water as needed or by diverting the hotter flow to let a pool cool down. The apparent local custom is clothing optional.

There are no services on the premises and camping is not permitted near the springs. However, there are three uncrowded Forest Service campgrounds within five miles of the Jerry Johnson Hot Springs trailhead. It is ten miles to a cafe, service station and all other services at Powell Junction.

Directions: Follow US 12 to Warm Springs Park bridge trailhead, which is located .5 miles west of mile marker 152. Park in a large area on the north side of US 12, walk over the bridge and follow FS 49, which is a two-person-wide path leading one mile southeast to the springs. Where the path forks, a narrow trail to the right leads down a series of primitive steps to the creek, where hot water tumbles into several creekside rock pools. Or, continue straight on the path to an open meadow to several groups of shallow soaking pools. When coming from the west on US 12, the trailhead for the springs is 77 miles from Lowell, 170 miles from Lewiston. Coming from the east, the trailhead is approximately 22.5 miles west of Lolo Pass at the Idaho-Montana state line, 55 mile west of Lolo and 63 miles southwest of Missoula, Montana.

Source map: *Clearwater National Forest*.

Editor's prerogative: While I generally like to see a hot spring with someone in it, I prefer to see this high-meadow pool at *Jerry Johnson* with no one in it and imagine myself there. Truly, one of my favorites.

Jerry Johnson Hot Springs: While mom and baby enjoy themselves in one of the pools that spread across the flats, the man in the photo, above right, is soaking in one of the riverside pools with a wonderful view along Warm Springs Creek.

406   BARTH HOT SPRINGS

● **West of the town of North Fork**

A truly unexpected, claw-footed bathtub in a remote section of the main Salmon River known as the River of No Return. Elevation 2,700 feet. Open all year, but access is extremely difficult in the winter because the Salmon River freezes over.

Natural mineral water flows out of many small seeps at temperatures up to 140° and cools as it is gathered into a PVC pipe carrying it to the outdoor bathtub. River guides have also constructed a rock and sand soaking pool. There are no posted clothing requirements, which leaves that matter up to the mutual consent of those present.

There are no services available on the premises, nor are there any roads to this area. Access is by raft or jet boat. It is 22 miles to the nearest road and 65 miles to all services.

The Forest Service issues licenses to a limited number of outfitters who operate raft and boat trips on an individual seat and charter basis. For more information, write to Idaho Outfitter's and Guides Association, Inc., Peck, Idaho, 83545.

Source maps: Forest Service, *The Salmon, River of No Return.*

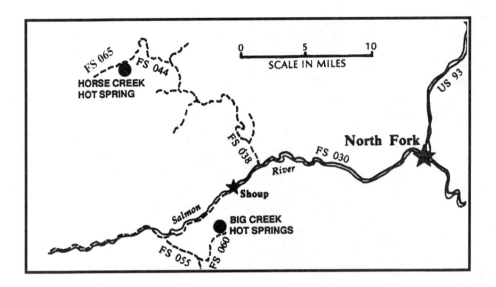

407   HORSE CREEK HOT SPRING
(see map)

●   **Northwest of the town of North Fork**

Rock-lined, primitive hot spring enclosed by four walls in a very remote section of beautiful Salmon National Forest. Elevation 6,200 feet. Open during summer months, depending on snowmelt.

Natural mineral water flows out of a spring at 97° and directly into the pool, which is surrounded by a roofless bathhouse. The apparent local custom is clothing optional.

Rest rooms, and a picnic area with table are available at the springs. It is one mile to a campground and 35 miles to all other services.

Directions: From the town of North Fork, go west on FS 030, north on FS 038, west and north on FS 044, then west and south on FS 065 to the spring.

Source map: *Salmon National Forest*.

The enclosure around the pool may keep the elements out, but it also means that while you sit and soak you can't see the beautiful view.

408   BIG CREEK HOT SPRINGS
(see map on facing page)

● West of the town of North Fork

Large, waist-deep pool fed by dozens of geothermal outflows along Warm Springs Creek in a remote, rocky canyon in Salmon National Forest. Elevation 4,800 feet. Open all year.

Natural mineral water emerges from a rocky hillside at 185° and flows toward the rock and cement pool built by the Sterlings in 1987 and also through other small pools in the creekbed. Cold water is scarce, so pool temperatures must be controlled by diverting the hot water flow as needed. There is also a rock sauna at the end of a steep primitive road that may not be safe when wet. There are no services available on the premises. It is 33 miles to all services in North Fork.

Source maps: *Salmon National Forest*; USGS *Shoup, Idaho-Montana*.

Volunteers spent a great deal of effort to edge the pools with rock and cement and also to carry the rocks uphill from the pool and build a sauna over a steam vent—look carefully, for it looks like just another rock pile.

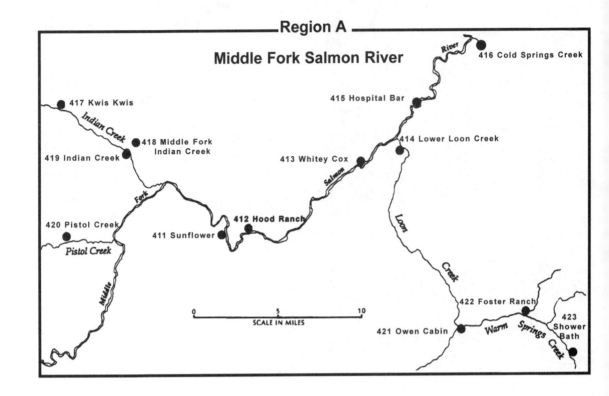

Region A

Middle Fork Salmon River

416 Cold Springs Creek

417 Kwis Kwis

415 Hospital Bar

418 Middle Fork Indian Creek

414 Lower Loon Creek

419 Indian Creek

413 Whitey Cox

420 Pistol Creek

412 Hood Ranch

411 Sunflower

Pistol Creek

SCALE IN MILES
0   5   10

422 Foster Ranch

423 Shower Bath

421 Owen Cabin

MIDDLE FORK SALMON RIVER HOT SPRINGS—BY RAFT OR TRAIL

To reach these springs, you can plan a rugged backpack route that will take you to several springs over a two- or three-day period. You can also find packaged river-raft trips, featuring hot springs on the Middle Fork of the Salmon. These tours fly you to an upriver air strip, provide rafts and all your gear, and stop at a hot springs every day. Clothed or clothing-optional trips can be planned. Several of our readers have had success with River Odysseys West, PO Box 579, Coeur d'Alene, ID 838114; (800) 451-6034.

The first step to rowing down the river, is to get to the river. This means that you and all your gear need to be flown into the area where the boats and the rest of the equipment is waiting for you.

411   SUNFLOWER FLATS HOT SPRINGS

(see map on page 90)

Natural mineral water from a group of hot springs (109°) flows through some shallow, cliff-top pools before dropping to the river's edge in the form of a hot waterfall.

412   HOOD RANCH HOT SPRINGS

(see map on page 90)

The geothermal water from springs with temperatures up to 149° cools as it flows through pipes to a crude shower-bath and soaking pool within 100 yards of the river.

413   WHITEY COX HOT SPRINGS
(see map on page 90)

●

A beautiful riverside meadow contains several classic, natural soaking pools supplied from nearby hot springs (131°) through channels where the water cools on the way.

414   LOWER LOON CREEK HOT SPRINGS
(see map on page 90)

●

A large, log soaking pool on the edge of Loon Creek is supplied by several springs with temperatures up to 120°. This pool does require a .25-mile hike from the raft-landing beach where the creek joins the river.

415   HOSPITAL BAR HOT SPRINGS
(see map on page 90)

●

Dozens of fissures in rocks along the riverbank emit 115°-geothermal water that is collected for soaking in a few shallow pools next to a favorite landing spot for rafts.

The boat landing at *Hospital Bar* is almost next to the hot springs themselves—a series of shallow pools right next to the river.

Playing croquet in this situation can really be called mixed doubles!

On this raft trip there were many areas of swift rapids. Some of the boaters actually fell in, but when things were calm, it was possible to pull out the kayaks and paddle around. After a long day on the river, plus a wonderful soak each day, everyone could count on a delicious dinner (how about Cornish game hens?) and a great night's sleep.

The ruins of Mormon Ranch are on the way up the hill to *Cold Creek Hot Spring*.

416   COLD SPRINGS CREEK HOT SPRING
(see map on page 90)

●

Located a mile from the river, this spring emits 140°-mineral water that flows first into a cooling pond and then is piped to this cozy soaking box.

WILDERNESS HOT SPRINGS—BY TRAIL ONLY
The creeks on which these springs are located are too narrow to negotiate by raft. Walk-in trails to these springs are described in Evie Litton's book, *The Hiker's Guide to Hot Springs in the Pacific Northwest,* Falcon Press, 1993. (Their locations are marked on the map on page 90.)

A beautiful view of the typical terrain visible along the Middle Fork Salmon River.

417   KWIS KWIS HOT SPRINGS

- Outflow temperature—156°

418   MIDDLE FORK INDIAN CREEK HOT SPRINGS

- Outflow temperature—162°

419   INDIAN CREEK HOT SPRINGS

- Outflow temperature—190°

420   PISTOL CREEK HOT SPRINGS

- Outflow temperature—115°

421   OWEN CABIN HOT SPRINGS

- Outflow temperature—133°

422   FOSTER RANCH HOT SPRINGS

- Outflow temperature—135°

423   SHOWER BATH HOT SPRINGS

- Outflow temperature—122°

Records show that water rights were filed as far back as 1876. At its peak in the late 1930s, the resort had a large, elegant lodge with dance halls and two large pools. The owners are in the process of restoring "one of the finest resorts in the state."

425 SALMON HOT SPRING
RR 1 PO Box 223 B (208) 756-4449
Salmon, ID 83467

Rustic rural plunge with a colorful past and history dating back over 100 years, currently undergoing major renovation while remaining open to the public on a day-use fee basis. Elevation 4,950 feet. Open all year.

Natural mineral water flows abundantly out of a spring 100 yards uphill at a temperature of 115° and is piped to a large outdoor recreational swimming pool that is maintained at 98° to 102°. (The indoor therapy pool is under restoration.) The flow-through pool is drained and refilled nightly, so no chemical treatment of the water is needed and there is no sulphur smell. Bathing suits are required.

Dressing rooms and snacks are available on the premises. There are several tepees for overnight rental and ample level ground for tent camping and self-contained RVs. It is eight miles to all other services in Salmon. Visa and MasterCard are accepted.

Directions: From Salmon, drive four miles south on US 93, turn left on Airport Road and drive .8 miles to a "T" intersection. Turn left again and follow Warm Springs Creek Road 3.5 miles to the spring.

426 SHARKEY HOT SPRING

● East of Salmon

A cozy wooden soaking box is all that remains of an old sheepherder's bathhouse in an open sagebrush canyon above the Lemhi Valley. Elevation 5,300 feet. Open all year.

Natural mineral water flows out of a spring at 105° directly into the four-foot by four-foot by two-foot box. The apparent local custom is clothing optional.

There are no services on the premises. It is 23 miles to all services.

Directions: From Salmon, drive east on ID28 to the Tendoy store. Turn left, go .2 miles and turn left again on Tendoy Lane. Drive three miles and turn right onto Warm Springs Wood Road. Follow this dirt road for two miles to the high voltage power line. Park just before crossing the bridge and walk 100 yards up a grassy trail to the spring.

Source map: *Salmon National Forest.*

Sharkey Hot Spring has one of the many soaking boxes found in Idaho, that usually indicate the remains of some back-country soak for miners or cowboys.

This pool has a view that goes on forever. Another of the pools provides a wonderful shower, and a third offers a place to put up your feet and enjoy the view or read a good book.

427 GOLDBUG HOT SPRINGS

● **Southwest of the town of Salmon**

Many delightful pools and cascades of various temperatures at the end of a steep, two-mile trail up a beautiful canyon in Salmon National Forest. Elevation 5,200 feet. Open all year.

Natural mineral water flows out of several springs at temperatures up to 110° and combines with cold creek water as it tumbles down the canyon. Volunteers have added rock-and-sand dams to deepen the water-worn cascade pools. Temperatures in these cascade pools are determined by the rate of cold water runoff. Some of the pools offer a spectacular view down the canyon. The apparent local custom is clothing optional.

There are no services available on the premises. Parking is available at the trailhead, and it is one mile to other services in Elk Bend.

Directions: On US 93 approximately 23 miles south of Salmon, look for mile marker 282. Go east on a short gravel road to the trailhead parking area. This parking lot is adjacent to private property. Cross the footbridge over Warm Springs Creek and follow the often steep trail up the canyon to the springs near the top of the ridge.

428   CHALLIS HOT SPRINGS
H/C 63 Box 1779   (208) 879-4442
■   **Challis, ID 83226**

Historic community plunge and campground on the banks of the Salmon River. Elevation 5,000 feet. Pools open all year; campground open April 1 to November.

Natural mineral water flows from several springs at temperatures up to 127° and is piped to flow-through indoor and outdoor pools that require no chemical treatment. The temperature of the outdoor pool is maintained at approximately 90°, and the temperature of the indoor pool ranges from 108-110°. Bathing suits are required.

Changing rooms, picnic areas, camping and RV hookups are available on the premises and seven miles to all other services. Visa and MasterCard are accepted.

Directions: From the intersection of US 93 and ID 75 near Challis, go southeast on US 93 and watch for signs to the hot springs.

429 BARNEY HOT SPRINGS

● **Northeast of the town of Challis**

A large warm pond located in a remote and scenic valley (BLM land) in the middle of the high desert, with a magnificent view of two mountain ranges. Elevation 6,400 feet. Open all year; road not maintained in winter.

Natural mineral water flows into the pond from a spring at one end of the pool. The 83° water fills the very large, four-foot-deep pond. The pool is visible from the road, so bathing suits are advisable.

There are no services available on the premises. It is .5 miles to Summit Creek Campground and 65 miles to all other services in Challis.

Directions: From Challis, drive north on Hwy 93 17 miles to Ellis. Turn east toward May and Patterson on the Pahsimeroi Road. Follow this road about 25 miles past Patterson to Summit Creek Campground. The pool is .5 miles past the campground on the opposite side of the road.

Source maps: USGS *Gilmore*; *Challis National Forest* (East).

Barney Hot Springs should probably be called Barney Warm Springs, but the location and views are wonderful and the cooler water temperature would feel refreshing during the hot days of summer.

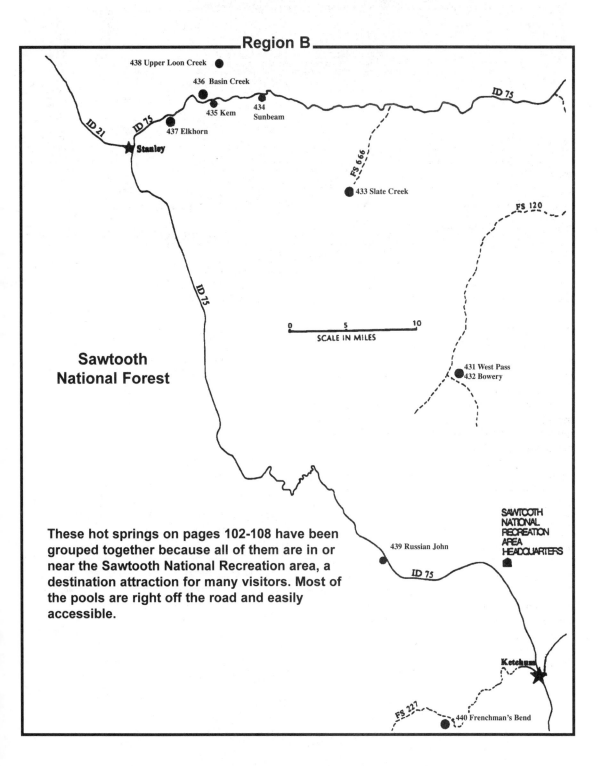

438 Upper Loon Creek

436 Basin Creek

435 Kem

434 Sunbeam

437 Elkhorn

ID 21

ID 75

Stanley

FS 666

433 Slate Creek

FS 120

ID 75

0   5   10
SCALE IN MILES

Sawtooth
National Forest

431 West Pass
432 Bowery

These hot springs on pages 102-108 have been grouped together because all of them are in or near the Sawtooth National Recreation area, a destination attraction for many visitors. Most of the pools are right off the road and easily accessible.

439 Russian John

SAWTOOTH
NATIONAL
RECREATION
AREA
HEADQUARTERS

ID 75

Ketchum

FS 227

440 Frenchman's Bend

The bathtub at *Bowery Hot Spring* overlooks the rock-edged pool that is located down by the river's edge.

431 WEST PASS HOT SPRING

● **Southeast of the town of Stanley**

A pair of out-in-the-open bathtubs along West Pass Creek, near an abandoned mine in Sawtooth National Recreation Area. Elevation 7,000 feet. Road closed December 1 to May 1.

Natural mineral water flows out of a grassy hillside at 105° and runs continuously through a hose to the ancient bathtubs, which maintain a temperature of 102°. The apparent local custom is clothing optional.

There are no services on the premises. There is a walk-in campground within two miles and a drive-in campground within 30 miles. It is 34 miles to all other services in Clayton.

Directions: From ID 75, four miles east of Clayton, drive south on FS 120 along the East Fork of the Salmon River 29 miles to West Pass Creek. Cross the creek, drive .3 miles uphill and park on the flat area. Hike down a trail 20 yards past the abandoned mine to the springs.

Source map: *Sawtooth National Recreation Area.*

432 BOWERY HOT SPRING

● **Southeast of the town of Stanley**

An outdoor bathtub and a rock-and-sand soaking pool on the edge of the South Fork of the Salmon River in the Sawtooth National Recreation Area. Elevation 6,800 feet. Road closed December 1 to May 1.

Natural mineral water flows out of a spring at 125° and through a hose to the tub and the pool. Water temperature in the tub is controlled by diverting the hot water inflow. Water temperature in the volunteer-built primitive pool is controlled by admitting cold river water. The apparent local custom is clothing optional.

There are no services on the premises. There is a walk-in campground within two miles and a drive-in campground within 30 miles. It is 34 miles to all other services in Clayton.

Directions: From ID 75, four miles east of Clayton, drive south on FS 120 along the East Fork of the Salmon River 30 miles to the parking lot at a trailhead. Hike 100 yards up the service road toward Bowery Forest Service Station. At the bridge, follow a trail upstream 100 yards to the spring.

433   SLATE CREEK HOT SPRING

● **Southeast of the town of Stanley**

A wooden soaking box and two rock-and-sand pools in a wooded canyon in the Sawtooth National Recreation Area. Elevation 7,000 feet. Open all year.

Natural mineral water flows out of a spring at 122° and through a hose to the box, which is all that remains of a bathhouse that once stood near the HooDoo mine. Another hose brings cold water, permitting complete control of the water temperature in the box. There are also two primitive pools on the edge of the creek. The apparent local custom is clothing optional.

There are no services available on the premises. It is 17 miles to gas and a convenience store and 30 miles to all other services.

Directions: Drive 23 miles east of Stanley on ID 75. Turn right on FS 666 (Slate Creek Road) and drive 7.4 miles along Slate Creek to a closed gate at the HooDoo mine entrance. Park and walk up the road the remaining 500 yards to the spring.

Source map: *Sawtooth National Recreation Area*.

What would the miners have done without the hot-springs bathhouses that dotted the Idaho landscape? All that's left today is the soaking box, although there are also pools down by the creek.

434   SUNBEAM HOT SPRINGS

● **East of the town of Stanley**

A bathing box and several rock-and-sand pools on the edge of the Salmon River in Challis National Forest. Elevation 6,000 feet. Open all year.

Natural mineral water flows out of several springs on the north side of the road at temperatures up to 160°. The water flows under the road to several volunteer-built rock pools along the north bank of the river (upstream from the parking lot), where hot and cold water mix in a variety of temperatures; a bathing box is located downstream from the parking area. As all pools are easily visible from the road, bathing suits are advisable.

A new toilet large enough to use as a changing room has recently been built and, except for the campgrounds, there are no other services on the premises. It is seven miles to all other services.

Location: On ID 75, one mile west of Sunbeam Resort, northeast of the town of Stanley.

435   KEM (BASIN CREEK BRIDGE) HOT SPRINGS

● **East of the town of Stanley**

Small, primitive spring and soaking pools on the edge of the Salmon River in Sawtooth National Recreation Area. Elevation 6,000 feet. Open all year.

Natural mineral water flows out of a spring at 110° and cools as it flows through several volunteer-built, rock-and-sand soaking pools along the edge of the river. Pool temperatures may be controlled by diverting the hot water or by bringing a bucket for adding cold river water. Because the spring is at the east end of a popular, unofficial campground, bathing suits are advisable in the daytime unless you check the situation out with your neighbors.

The adjoining camping area is primitive with no services on the premises. It is seven miles to all services.

Directions: On ID 75, 0.7 of a mile east of mile marker 197, turn off the highway toward the river and down a short gravel road into the camping area.

Source map: *Sawtooth National Recreation Area* (hot springs not shown).

436   BASIN CREEK CAMPGROUND HOT SPRING

● **East of the town of Stanley**

Several shallow pools located on the edge of a creek adjacent to a campground in the Sawtooth National Recreation Area. Elevation 6,000 feet. Open all year.

Natural mineral water at 137° flows out of the ground and is mixed with cold creek water before flowing into several volunteer rock-and-sand pools. It is advisable to wear a bathing suit as the pools are near the campground.

There is an adjoining campground, and it is seven miles to all other services in Stanley.

Directions: Drive seven miles east of Stanley to Basin Creek Campground. Walk from campsite #4 through the bushes to the creek. The pools are hidden on the opposite side.

Source map: *Sawtooth National Forest* (hot springs not shown).

If one box was fun then two would be even better. At least that's what the person who built the second box must have been thinking. Be sure to bring a bucket to add cold river water to the box if you want to soak—the tub water is hot!

437 ELKHORN (BOAT BOX) HOT SPRING

● **East of the town of Stanley**

Small, wood soaking boxes perched on a rock between the road and the Salmon River in the Sawtooth National Recreation Area. Elevation 6,100 feet. Open all year.

Natural mineral water flows out of a spring at 136° and is piped under the road to two soaking boxes. The temperature in the boxes is regulated by diverting the flow of hot water and pouring in buckets of cold river water. Bathing suits are advisable as the location is visible from the road.

There are no services on the premises. It is one mile to the Salmon River Campground and two miles to all services.

Directions: On ID 75, 0.7 of a mile east of mile marker 192, watch for a small turnout (two car limit) on the river side of the road. The box is visible from the turnout.

Source map: *Sawtooth National Recreation Area* (hot springs not shown).

438   UPPER LOON CREEK
HOT SPRINGS
(see map)

● **Northeast of the town of Stanley**

A series of beautiful springs on the east side of Upper Loon Creek in the Salmon River Mountains in the beautifully wooded hills of the Frank Church Wilderness Area. Elevation 5,100 feet. Closes early and opens late, depending on snowfall.

Natural mineral water from several springs on a hillside above the creek flows at temperatures around 145° down the rock cliffs and into the pools at the edge of the creek. At the camping area there are several rock-and-sand pools that receive their hot water from slow-flowing seeps across the ground. The water temperature in the pools can be adjusted by mixing in cold creek water. The apparent local custom is clothing optional.

There are no services on the premises, but there are informal spaces to pitch a tent, including one near the remains of a log cabin. The nearest campground, Tin Cup, is 6.5 miles away. It is 40 miles to all other services in Stanley.

Directions: From Stanley, drive east on ID 75 13 miles to Sunbeam. Follow FS 013 north about seven miles and bear left on FS 172. Follow FS 172 over Loon Creek Summit to the Loon Creek Ranger Station. Turn right on FS 007 and follow it to the end of the road and the trailhead. Tin Cup campground is less than a mile from the end of the road. The easy hike to the springs is about 5.5 miles. Look for an old cabin between the trail and the river. There are pools near the cabin, but the best ones are a few hundred yards downstream. The road is poor and not recommended for motor homes or large trailers.

Source Maps: *Challis National Forest* (West); USGS *Rock Creek*.

While the season may be short, this spot is certainly a gem to visit. At 11.5 miles round trip, an overnight stay would seem a good idea and part of the pleasure would be early and late soaks in the beautiful pool below the waterfall. What a fabulous place to watch a full moon light the sky.

440   FRENCHMAN'S BEND HOT SPRING

● **West of the town of Ketchum**

Several primitive roadside pools along both banks of Warm Springs Creek. Elevation 6,400 feet. Open all year for day use only.

Natural mineral water flows from the ground at more than 120° and into volunteer-built rock-and-sand pools where it is mixed with cold creek water to produce a comfortable soaking temperature. Nudity, alcohol, glass containers, non-biodegradable soap or shampoo and littering are prohibited.

There are no services on the premises. Roadside parking limitations must be observed. It is 11 miles to all services.

Directions: From ID 75 (Main Street) in Ketchum, drive 10.7 miles west on Warm Springs Road. Park in the well-marked parking area and walk 200 yards upstream to the spring.

Source Map: *Sawtooth National Recreation Area.*

439   RUSSIAN JOHN HOT SPRING

● **North of the town of Ketchum**

Remains of an old sheepherder's soaking pool on a slope 200 yards above the highway in Sawtooth National Recreation Area. Elevation 6,900 feet. Open all year.

Natural mineral water flows out of a spring at 89° and directly into a small, clay-bottom pool that maintains a temperature of no more than 86°. Despite the cool temperature, this pool is so popular you may have to wait your turn. The apparent local custom is clothing optional.

There are no services available on the premises. It is 18 miles to all services.

Directions: On ID 75, 30 yards south of mile marker 146, turn west and then south to the parking area.

Source map: *Sawtooth National Recreation Area.*

441   WILD ROSE HOT SPRINGS

● **East of the town of Carey**

An abundance of wild roses near this rock-and-gravel pool give it its name. The area is surrounded by lava flows to the south and sparsely covered hills to the north. Elevation 5,000 feet. Open all year.

A natural mineral water spring flows over marshy ground at 99° to an 8 by 15-foot pool, up to three-feet deep and made of lava rock with a gravel bottom. The springs are located on BLM land, but the pool is on private land. Please use, but don't abuse. Bathing suits are advisable.

There are no services on the premises. It is 15.5 miles to a campground at Craters of the Moon National Monument and 34 miles to all other service in Arco.

Directions: From Carey, drive 10 miles east on Highway 20-26-93. One-half mile east of mile marker 214, look for a small turnout on the north side of the road. Park and follow the trail north toward the hill. It's about 100 yards to the pool.

Map Sources: BLM *Craters of the Moon*; USGS *Paddleford Flat*.

442   WORSWICK HOT SPRINGS

● **East of the town of Featherville**

Dozens of primitive springs send a large flow of geothermal water tumbling down several acres of rolling hillside in the Sawtooth National Forest. Elevation 6,400 feet. Open all year.

Natural mineral water flows out of many springs at temperatures of more than 150°, supplying a series of volunteer-built, rock-and-log pools in the drainage channels. The water cools as it flows downhill, so the lower the pool, the lower the temperature. The apparent local custom is clothing optional.

There are no services available on the premises. It is two miles to overnight camping and 14 miles to all other services.

Directions: From the town of Featherville, go east on FS 227 to the intersection with FS 094, then 2.2 miles farther on FS 227.

Source map: *Sawtooth National Forest*.

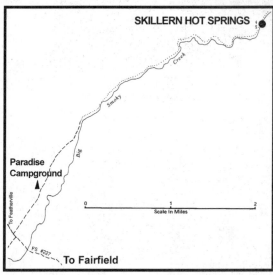

SKILLERN HOT SPRINGS

Paradise Campground

To Featherville

Big

Smoky

Creek

Scale In Miles

FS #227

To Fairfield

444　SKILLERN HOT SPRINGS

(see map)

● **East of the town of Featherville**

Primitive hot spring on Big Smokey Creek, three miles by trail from Canyon Campground. Elevation 5,800 feet. Open all year.

Natural mineral water flows south from a spring at more than 110°, supplying a volunteer-built rock pool at the creek's edge. Pool temperature is controllable by varying the amount of cold creek water admitted. The local custom is clothing optional.

There are no services on the premises. It is three miles to the campground and trailhead and 24 miles to all other services.

Directions: From Featherville, go 21 miles east on FS 227 to FS 072 and turn north to Canyon Campground. Trailhead is at the north end of the campground. The trail fords the stream several times and might not be passable during high water.

Source maps: *Sawtooth National Forest*; USGS *Sydney Butte and Paradise Peak, Idaho.*

443　PREIS HOT SPRING

● **East of the town of Featherville**

Small, two-person soaking box near the side of the road in Sawtooth National Forest. Elevation 6,000 feet. Open all year.

Natural mineral water flows out of the spring at 94° and directly into a small pool that has been given board sides and is large enough to accommodate two very friendly soakers. Bathing suits are advisable.

There are no services on the premises. It is two miles to overnight camping and 14 miles to all other services.

Directions: From the town of Featherville, go east on FS 227 to the intersection with FS 072, then 3.3 miles farther on FS 227. Watch for spring 10 yards from the north side of the road.

Source map: *Sawtooth National Forest.*

445   BAUMGARTNER HOT SPRINGS

• **East of the town of Featherville**

Well-maintained soaking pool in popular Baumgartner Campground in Sawtooth National Forest. Elevation 5,000 feet. Open all year for day use only.

Natural mineral water flows out of a spring at 108°, supplying the soaking pool on a flow-through (no chlorine) basis and maintaining the temperature at 105°. Because of the pool's location in a campground, bathing suits are required.

Campground facilities are on the premises. It is 11 miles to a motel, restaurant, service station and grocery store, and 48 miles to RV hookups.

Location: On FS 227, 11 miles east of Featherville.

Source map: *Sawtooth National Forest.*

While there's a fee for camping, a soak in this very well-maintained pool is free. The National Forest Service does a good job of keeping the pool clean on a daily basis.

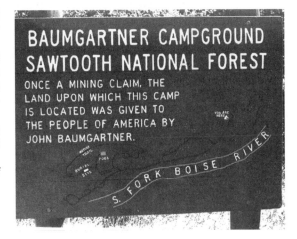

The lower pools at *Willow Creek* are the only ones left after a forest fire destroyed the volunteer-built upper pools. By the time you get there, someone may have already rebuilt them.

446   WILLOW CREEK HOT SPRINGS

● **East of the town of Featherville**

A series of primitive soaking pools in a lovely, small alpine valley in the Sawtooth National Forest. Elevation 5,200 feet. Open all year.

Natural mineral water flows out of the ground at 125° and runs 100 yards across a gravel bar to join the creek. Volunteers have built a large rock-and-sand soaking pool where the water cools to 105° and a smaller one where the water cools to 96°. The apparent local custom is clothing optional.

There are no services available at the spring, but there is a campground at the trailhead. It is 10 miles to other services in Featherville, and 47 miles to RV hookups.

Directions: From Featherville, drive seven miles east on FS 227 to Willow Creek, then two miles north on FS 008 to the campground and trailhead. The spring is .75 miles north on a moderate, well-maintained trail.

Source map: *Sawtooth National Forest.*

447   JOHNSON'S BRIDGE HOT SPRING

● **North of the town of Pine**

Popular series of pools at the edge of the Boise River, both at the north and south ends of the bridge. Elevation 4,400 feet. Open all year.

Natural mineral water flows out of the springs on the bank above the river. The 135° water flows through natural channels to the rock-and-sand pools at the river's edge. Several of the pools are at the north end of the bridge crossing, and there is a single pool just below the south bridge abutment. The water temperature can be controlled by mixing the hot water with cold river water. Bathing suits are required.

The springs are adjacent to Elks Flat Campground. It is 4.5 miles to gas in Pine and five miles to all other services in Featherville.

Directions: Drive 4.5 miles north of Pine to the campground and bridge.

Source Maps: *Boise National Forest*; USGS *Featherville.*

Johnson's Bridge Hot Spring: These riverside pools are found at the north end of the bridge, and there is also one pool just below the south bridge abutment.

450   GREEN CANYON HOT SPRINGS
■   **Box 96**   **(208) 458-4454**
     Newdale, ID 83436

Rural, indoor plunge and RV park in a really green canyon. Elevation 6,000 feet. Open every day except Sunday from mid-April to the end of September; open weekends the rest of the year.

Natural mineral water flows out of a spring at 118° and is piped to pools and a geothermal greenhouse. The indoor swimming pool is maintained at 90°, and the outdoor hydrojet pool is maintained at 105°. Both pools are treated with chlorine, and bathing suits are required.

Locker rooms, snack bar, picnic area, and RV hookups are available on the premises. It is 21 miles to all other services. No credit cards are accepted.

Directions: From the town of Driggs, go north and west 17 miles on ID 33. At Canyon Creek bridge, turn south and follow signs four miles to the resort.

451   HEISE HOT SPRINGS

Box 417   **(208) 538-7312**

■   **Ririe, ID 83443**

Modernized, family-oriented resort with spacious, tree-shaded picnic and RV grounds on the north bank of the Snake River. Elevation 5,000 feet. Open all year except the month of November.

Natural mineral water flows out of a spring at 126° and is piped to an enclosed hydrojet pool that is maintained at 105° and requires no chemical treatment. Tap water, treated with chlorine and heated by geothermal heat exchangers, is used in the other pools. An outdoor soaking pool is maintained at 92-93°, the large swimming pool at 82°, and the water-slide pick-up pool at 85°. Bathing suits are required in all areas.

Locker rooms, cafe, overnight camping, RV hookups, picnic area, and golf course are available on the premises. It is five miles to a store, service station, and motel. No credit cards are accepted.

Directions: From the town of Idaho Falls, go east 22 miles on US 26 and then follow signs four miles north across the river to the resort.

452A LAVA HOT SPRINGS FOUNDATION
PO Box 669 (800) 423-8597
■ **Lava Hot Springs, ID 83246**

Two attractive and well-maintained recreation areas operated by a self-supporting state agency in the town of Lava Hot Springs. Elevation 5,000 feet.

GEOTHERMAL POOLS: (East end of town; open 363 days per year.) Natural mineral water flows out of the ground at 112° and directly up through the gravel bottoms of a Roman-style pool in a sunken garden and of a large, partly shaded soaking pool. No chemical treatment is necessary. Pool temperatures range as low as 107° at the drain end of the soaking pool. The same water is pumped to two partly shaded hydrojet pools where cold shower water may be added to control the pool temperature. Bathing suits are required. Massage is available on the premises.

SWIMMING POOLS: (West end of town; open Memorial Day to Labor Day.) Hot mineral water is piped from the geothermal springs and flows continuously through the TAC-size pool and the Olympic-size pool, maintaining a temperature of 80°. The pool complex is surrounded by a large, level lawn. Bathing suits are required.

Locker rooms are available at both locations, and it is less than three blocks to all other services. No credit cards are accepted.

The pools (above) at *Lava Hot Springs* (east) offer several choices as to temperature. The hot tub below at the *Riverside Inn* offers a view of the Portneuf River.

452B   RIVERSIDE INN
255 Portneuf Ave.   (800) 733-5504
■ **Lava Hot Springs, ID 83246**

A faithfully restored historic hotel built originally in 1914, and once known as the Elegant Grand Inn, picturesquely situated on the banks of the Portneuf River. Close by to summer and winter recreation areas. Elevation 5,400 feet. Open all year.

Natural mineral water is pumped out of a well at 133°, diluted with cold water down to 104°, then piped to two small, and one large indoor private soaking pools and one outdoor soaking pool overlooking the river. Because the pools operate on a continuous flow-through basis, no chemical treatment of the water is needed. The pools are available to the public as well as to registered guests.

Fourteen nonsmoking rooms and suites, most with a private bath, are available on the premises. All other services are within three blocks. Major credit cards are accepted. Phone for rates and information.

452C   HOME HOTEL AND MOTEL
306 E. Main   (208) 776-5507
■ **Lava Hot Springs, ID 83246**

Remodeled, older hotel featuring hot mineral baths in all units, on the main street between the two Lava Hot Springs Foundation locations (see page 115). Elevation 5,400 feet. Open all year.

Natural mineral water flows out of a spring at 121° and is piped to two-person tubs in all rooms and in a rental house. Temperature in each tub is controllable by the customer. The eight rooms in the hotel are non-smoking; the 13 rooms in the motel section permit smoking.

It is less than three blocks to a cafe, store, service station, overnight camping, and RV hookups. Visa and MasterCard are accepted.

453 RIVERDALE RESORT
3696 N. 1600 E.   **(208) 852-0266**
■ **Preston, ID 83263**

New commercial development in a rural valley subdivision. Elevation 4,000 feet. Open all year.

Natural mineral water is pumped from a geothermal well at 112°, then piped to various outdoor pools. All soaking pools are flow-through and drained daily, eliminating the need for chemical treatment of the water. The partly shaded hydrojet pool is maintained at 103-105°, and a large soaking pool is maintained at 97-100° in the summer and 102-104° in the winter. The chlorinated junior Olympic swimming pool is maintained at 86° in the summer. A chlorinated waterslide catch pool is maintained at approximately 80°. Bathing suits are required.

A new eight-unit bed and breakfast with whirlpool tubs is a recent addition to the modern hotel rooms, all of which are non-smoking rooms. Locker rooms, snack bar, overnight camping, and RV hookups are available on the premises. It is less than six miles to a cafe, store, service station, and motel. Visa and MasterCard are accepted.

Directions: From Preston on US 91, go six miles north on ID 34 and watch for the resort signs.

454 DOWNATA HOT SPRINGS
25901 Downata Rd. (208) 897-5736
■ **Downey, ID 83234**

Expanded, older, rural plunge and picnic grounds in the rolling hills of southeastern Idaho. Elevation 4,000 feet. Open Memorial Day to Labor Day.

Natural mineral water flows out of a spring at 112° and is piped to outdoor pools treated with chlorine. The main swimming pool and the waterslide catch pool are maintained at 85-95°, and a hot tub is maintained at 104°. Bathing suits are required.

Bed and breakfast, poolside restaurant, catering, child care, in addition to locker rooms, snack bar, picnic grounds, overnight camping, and volleyball court are all available on the premises. It is three miles to a store, service stations, and a motel. Major credit cards are accepted.

Directions: On US 91, drive 3 miles south from the town of Downey and watch for signs.

Bed and breakfast and child care make for a great vacation stop while you try out the various pools, slides, and unique tilting float located in the center of the main swimming pool.

455 INDIAN SPRINGS NATATORIUM
3249 Indian Springs Rd.
(208) 226-2174
■ **American Falls, ID 83211**

Older, rural picnic ground and plunge with RV accommodations. Elevation 5,200 feet. Open April 1 to Labor Day.

Natural mineral water flows out of a spring at 90° and is piped to an outdoor swimming pool that is treated with chlorine and maintains a temperature of 90°. Bathing suits are required.

Locker rooms, picnic area and full-hookup RV spaces are available on the premises. It is three miles to all other services. No credit cards are accepted.

Location: On Idaho Route 37, three miles south of the city of American Falls.

456   NAT-SOO-PAH HOT SPRINGS
2738 E. 2400 N.   (208) 655-4337
■   **Hollister, ID 83301**

Clean and quiet community plunge with soaking pools and acres of tree-shaded grass for picnics and overnight camping. Located on the Snake River plain, south of Twin Falls. Elevation 4,400 feet. Open May 1 to Labor Day.

Natural mineral water flows out of a spring at 99° and is piped to three outdoor pools. The swimming pool maintained at 92-94°, uses flow-through and some chlorine treatment. Part of the swimming pool flow-through is heated with a heat pump to supply the soaking pool, which is maintained at a temperature of 104-106°. The hydrojet pool, supplied by direct flow-through from the spring, maintains a temperature of 99° and requires no chemical treatment. There is also a small waterslide at the side of the swimming pool. Bathing suits are required.

Locker rooms, snack bar, picnic area, overnight camping, and RV hookups are available on the premises. It is four miles to a store and service station and 16 miles to a motel. No credit cards are accepted.

Directions: From US 93, .5 miles south of Hollister and .5 miles north of the Port of Entry, go east three miles on Nat-Soo-Pah Road directly to the location.

457A BANBURY HOT SPRINGS
■ Route 3, Box 48   (208) 543-4098
Buhl, ID 83316

Community plunge on the Snake River with soaking pools and a spacious, tree-shaded area for picnics and overnight camping. Elevation 3,000 feet. Open mid-May to Labor Day.

Natural mineral water flows out of a spring at 141° and is piped to a large, outdoor, chlorine-treated pool that is maintained at a temperature of 89-95°. Mineral water is also piped to five private-space soaking pools, some equipped with hydrojets. Water temperature in each pool is individually controlled. Each soaking pool is drained, cleaned, and refilled after each use, so that no chemical treatment of the water is needed. Bathing suits are required except in private-space pools.

Locker rooms, snack bar, overnight camping, RV hookups, and a boat ramp and dock are located on the premises. It is four miles to a restaurant and 12 miles to a store, service station, and motel. No credit cards are accepted.

Directions: From the town of Buhl, go 10 miles north on US 30. Watch for the sign and turn east 1.5 miles to the resort.

The water temperature in each of the indoor hot tubs is individually controlled and is drained after each use so no chlorine treatment is needed.

Soakers both young and old exercise to keep in shape by swimming and doing pull-ups on the bars.

457B MIRACLE HOT SPRINGS
Route 3 Box 171   (208) 543-6002
■ **Buhl, ID 83316**

Older health spa surrounded by rolling agricultural land. Elevation 3,000 feet. Open all year.

Natural mineral water is pumped out of a well at 139° and into an outdoor swimming pool and 19 roofless, enclosed soaking pools, all of which operate on a flow-through basis requiring no chemical treatment. The swimming pool is maintained at a temperature of 95°, and the temperature in the individual pools is controllable. Bathing suits are required in public areas. All buildings and dressing rooms are supplied with geothermal heat.

Massage by appointment, RV hookups, and overnight camping are available on the premises. A restaurant is available within three miles, and all other services are available within 10 miles. No credit cards are accepted.

Location: On US 30, 10 miles north of the town of Buhl.

Take the two people above and multiply that number by ten—that's how many people would fit comfortably in this indoor hydrojet pool.

458   SLIGAR'S THOUSAND SPRINGS RESORT

Route 1, Box 90   **(208) 837-4987**
■ **Hagerman, ID 83332**

Indoor plunge with private-space hydrojet tubs and green, shaded RV park with a view of multiple waterfalls on cliffs across the Snake River. Elevation 2,900 feet. Open all year.

Natural mineral water flows out of a spring at 200° and is piped to an indoor swimming pool, 17 indoor hydrojet pools large enough for eight people, and one indoor hydrojet pool large enough for 20 people. The temperature in the swimming pool is maintained between 90-96°, while the temperature in the hydrojet pools is individually controllable. All the pools are chlorinated. Bathing suits are required in public areas.

Locker rooms, boat dock, shaded picnic area, overnight camping, and RV hookups are available on the premises. A restaurant is within one mile, and all other services are within five miles. No credit cards are accepted.

Location: On US 30, eight miles south of the town of Hagerman.

459   MURPHY'S HOT SPRINGS
(208) 857-2233

■   **Rogerson, ID 83302**

Western-style pool, bathhouse, bar, and RV park in a remote section of the Jarbridge River Canyon. Elevation 5,100 feet. Open all year.

Natural mineral water flows out of two springs at 129° and into an outdoor, chlorine-treated pool and three indoor, flow-through soaking pools requiring no chemicals. The swimming pool is maintained at temperatures ranging from 80-90°. The large indoor pool for use by six people is maintained at 96°, and the two smaller, two-person tubs are maintained at 104° and 107°. Pools are open to the public in addition to registered guests. Bathing suits are required in the pool and public areas.

Dressing rooms, cafe, gas pump, cabins, overnight camping, and RV hookups are available on the premises. It is 49 miles to a store and service station. No credit cards are accepted.

Directions: From Twin Falls, go approximately 37 miles south on US 93. Watch for a highway sign and turn southwest .5 miles into Rogerson. At the main intersection, watch for Murphy Hot Springs highway sign and follow signs 49 miles to the location. Only the last few miles are on gravel road.

460   GIVENS HOT SPRINGS
HC79 Box 103   (208) 495-2000
■   Melba, ID 83641

Rural plunge, picnic grounds, and RV park on agricultural plateau above the Snake River. Elevation 3,000 feet. Open all year.

Natural mineral water flows out of an artesian spring at 120° and is piped to a chlorine-treated, indoor swimming pool and six indoor, private-space soaking pools that operate on a drain-and-fill basis requiring no chemicals. The swimming pool is maintained at a temperature of 99° in the winter and 85° in the summer. The temperature in the tubs is individually controllable, with temperatures ranging from 105-110°. Bathing suits are required.

Dressing rooms, snack bar, picnic grounds, softball diamond, and overnight camping are available on the premises. It is 11 miles to all other services. Visa and MasterCard are accepted.

Location: Eleven miles southeast of the town of Marsing on ID 78.

461 WARM SPRINGS RESORT
P.O. Box 28   **(208) 392-4437**
■   **Idaho City, ID 86361**

Rural plunge and RV park surrounded by Boise National Forest. Elevation 4,000 feet. Open all year.

Natural mineral water flows out of a spring at 110° and through an outdoor swimming pool maintained at a temperature of 94° in summer and 97° in winter. Chemical treatment of the water is not required. The pool is open to the public as well as to registered guests. Bathing suits are required.

Locker rooms, snack bar, cabins, overnight camping, and RV hookups are available on the premises. A cafe, store, and service station are located within two miles. No credit cards are accepted.

Location: On ID 21, 1.5 miles south of Idaho City.

Middle Fork Boise River

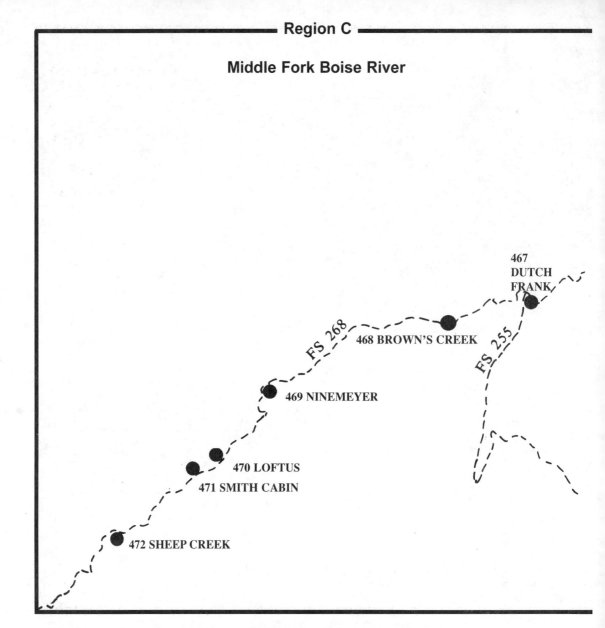

467
DUTCH
FRANK

FS 268

468 BROWN'S CREEK

FS 255

469 NINEMEYER

470 LOFTUS

471 SMITH CABIN

472 SHEEP CREEK

Middle Fork Boise River
Starting Point—town of Atlanta
Pages 128-133

Some of the springs in this area are open all year, weather permitting (these are noted). Many of the pools right on the river are submerged during spring runoff and are not available until mid-July; those requiring fording the river often are not available until mid-August. The season may last until early October.

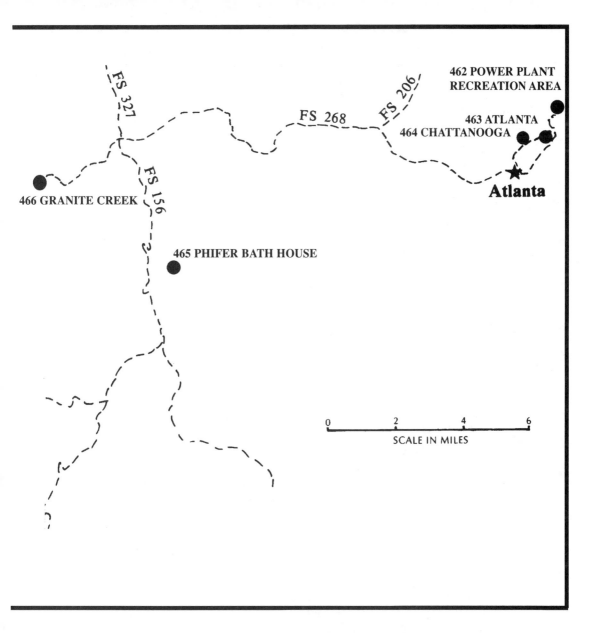

FS 327

FS 268

FS 206

462 POWER PLANT RECREATION AREA

463 ATLANTA

464 CHATTANOOGA

Atlanta

466 GRANITE CREEK

FS 156

465 PHIFER BATH HOUSE

```
0        2        4        6
SCALE IN MILES
```

    Depending on which route you use to get to Atlanta, and on your type of vehicle, make sure you fill your gas tank in Boise, Idaho City, or Featherville. A store and some accommodations are available in Atlanta, but no gas. Source maps for most of the springs (some springs are not shown) are *Boise National Forest*; USGS *Atlanta East* and *Atlanta West*.

462 POWER PLANT RECREATION AREA HOT SPRINGS
(see map on page 127)

● **Northeast of the town of Atlanta**

Several small pools adjacent to the Middle Fork of the Boise River and surrounded by wooded hillsides and open views of the Sawtooth Wilderness Area. Elevation 5,400 feet. Open all year.

Natural mineral water flows out of springs located near the river channel into several small, four- to six-foot pools, about a foot or so deep. As the pools are adjacent to the river, the water temperature can be regulated by adding river water but since the water temperature is only 100° this usually isn't necessary. The pools can be easily seen from the campground, so suits are recommended.

The pools are adjacent to Power Plant Campground, and all other services are 1.3 miles away in Atlanta.

Directions: Drive about 2.5 miles past Atlanta Hot Springs to the large flat "ball diamond" area at the entrance to the Power Plant Campground. The pools are located at the river's edge down a 25-foot embankment from the north end of the "ball diamond" area.

463 ATLANTA HOT SPRINGS
(see map on page 127)

● **Northeast of the town of Atlanta**

Rock-and-masonry soaking pool on a wooded plateau adjacent to a one-acre pond popular for summer swimming in the beautiful Sawtooth Mountains of Boise National Forest. Elevation 5,400 feet. Open all year; road access in winter could be difficult.

Natural mineral water flows out of a spring at 110° and cools as it travels to a nearby, volunteer-built pool, six feet by 12 feet, designed to be drained and quickly refilled after each use. The pool temperature is approximately 100°, depending on air temperature and wind conditions. The water drains into a large warm pond that locals call the "Frog Pond," which is used as a local swimming hole in the summer. This site is easily visible from the nearby road, so bathing suits are advisable.

No services are on the premises. It is .5 miles to the Power Plant Campground.

Directions: From Atlanta, follow FS 268 1.3 miles northwest. Pass a large pond on the right side of the road and park in a small turnout on the right side of the road immediately past the pond. The pool is visible from the parking area.

464   CHATTANOOGA HOT SPRINGS
(see map on page 127)

- **Northeast of the town of Atlanta**

Large, comfortable, sand-bottom pool at the foot of a geothermal cliff surrounded by the tree-covered slopes of Boise National Forest and a magnificent view of the Sawtooth Wilderness. Elevation 5,400 feet. Open all year.

Natural mineral water flows out of fissures in a 100-foot-high cliff at 120° and cools as it tumbles toward a volunteer-built, rock-and-sand soaking pool that retains a temperature of more than 100°. The apparent local custom is clothing optional.

There are no services on the premises. It is .75 miles to Power Point Campground.

Directions: From Atlanta follow FS268 a little over a mile northeast toward Power Plant Campground. At the top of a hill where a large pond and Atlanta Hot Springs are visible, look for a road to the left. Follow the road a short distance and park near the edge of a cliff. The pool is visible from the north edge of the unmarked parking area at the top of the cliff. Several well-worn, steep paths lead down about 100 feet to the pool.

The view from the top of the hill doesn't begin to show what you can find at the bottom—waterfalls, a large soaking area, and a wonderful view of the river.

465 PHIFER BATH HOUSE
(see map on page 127)

● **West of the town of Atlanta**

A scrap wood and plastic bathhouse set in the rugged mountains on the Middle Fork Boise River. Elevation 4,400 feet. Open all year; road access in winter could be difficult.

Natural mineral water flows out of a warm artesian well at 85° and is piped from the wellhead to the bath house that has a shower stall and tub. The apparent local custom is clothing optional.

It is eight miles to Queen's River Campground.

Directions: Drive 17 miles west of Atlanta on FS 268 to the intersection of FS 327 and FS 156. Follow FS 156 south over the bridge, crossing the Middle Fork Boise River and turning left on the first road. The short .25 mile road fords Phifer Creek and ends at the bathhouse.

466 GRANITE CREEK HOT SPRING
(see map on page 127)

● **West of the town of Atlanta**

Large, deep pool located between FS 268 and the Middle Fork Boise River surrounded by wooded hills and considered by some to be one of the best. Elevation 4,200 feet. Open seasonally.

Natural mineral water flows out of several springs with temperatures up to 130° and runs through channels to a 12-foot by 20-foot, waist-deep, rock-and-sand pool located on the river's edge. Cold water from the river can be added to the pool to control the temperature. The pools are close to the road, so suits are advisable.

There are no services on the premises, and it is 11 miles to Idaho Outdoor Association Campground.

Directions: Drive 3.5 miles west on FS 268 from the intersection of FS 237 and FS 156. Look for a large parking area cut into the hill on the right. The pool is easily visible from the road.

467   DUTCH FRANK (ROARING RIVER) HOT SPRINGS
(see map on page 126)

● **Southwest of the town of Atlanta**

Several small pools at the bottom of a canyon on the edge of the Middle Fork Boise River. Elevation 4,100 feet. Open seasonally.

Natural mineral water flows from many small springs along several hundred yards of shoreline at temperatures up to 150°. Natural channels disperse the water into several small rock-and-sand pools that can be mixed with river water to adjust the temperature. Pools are highly visible from the road, and swimsuits are advised.

There are no services on the premises and it is eight miles to the Idaho Outdoor Association Campground.

Directions: Drive west from Atlanta on FS 268 for 22 miles to the junction of FS 255 at Roaring River. Turn south and cross the Middle Fork Boise River on FS 255 to a small parking area. Walk a few hundred yards east to the highly visible thermal area.

468   BROWN'S CREEK HOT SPRING
(see map on page 126)

● **Southwest of the town of Atlanta**

Gorgeous photo-opportunity hot water shower on the opposite bank of the Middle Fork Boise River in a narrow canyon with steep hills and very fast water. This one is tricky to get to even at low water in late summer. Elevation 3,900 feet. Open seasonally.

Natural mineral water cascades from springs on a cliff above the pool at 120°, cooling as it flows down the cliff into a small six- by six-foot soaking pool at the base of the shower. The pool is easily visible from the road, and bathing suits are advised.

It is five miles to the Idaho Outdoor Association Campground.

Directions: From Atlanta, drive 25 miles west on FS 268 look for hot water flowing down the cliff on the south side of the river. Parking is available in a turnoff directly opposite the spring. The river is swift at this point and caution should be used when fording the river.

470   LOFTUS HOT SPRINGS
(see map on page 126)

● **Southwest of the town of Atlanta**

One of the more romantic spots with a warm shower, peaceful pools, and a grotto-like overhang lending a sense of privacy. Located above the road with a lovely view of the river and surrounding woods. Elevation 3,600 feet. Open all year.

Natural mineral water at 130° showers over the edge of an overhang into an eight-foot, very clean, sandy-bottom pool. The water in the upper pool, now at 105°, continues to flow into a lower six-foot pool supplied by the main pool runoff. The apparent local custom is clothing optional or by common consent.

Be aware: there is a great deal of poison oak, so watch where you put your towel.

It is four miles to Ninemeyer Campground.

Directions: From Atlanta, drive 34 miles west on FS 268. Look for a turnoff to the north and hot water flowing down the hill. The pools are a few yards up the hill from the parking area.

469   NINEMEYER HOT SPRINGS
(see map on page 126)

● **Southwest of the town of Atlanta**

Small pools on the south side of the Middle Fork Boise River across from a campground with a wonderful adjacent swimming hole. Elevation 3,700 feet. Open seasonally (late August to October).

Several springs at 169° flow gently down the hillside to a riverside rock-and-sand pool that is presently about six by eight feet. The pool can be cooled by adding river water. It is easily visible from the road, and bathing suits are advised.

The springs are at Ninemeyer Campground.

Directions: From Atlanta drive west on FS 268 about 30 miles to Ninemeyer Campground. Look for the steamy hillside and pools directly across the river from the campground.

Source Map: USGS *Barber Flats*.

471   SMITH CABIN HOT SPRINGS
(see map on page 126)

● **Southwest of the town of Atlanta**

Small rock pools on both sides of the Middle Fork Boise River. Elevation 3,500 feet. Open seasonally.

Natural mineral water flows out of the hillside above the river on the north bank and into volunteer-built, rock-and-sand pools on a gravel bar at the river's edge. On the south side, water flows to a small, shallow pool at the river's edge. These pools can only be accessed when the river is slow (mid-August) and are visible upstream from the ones on the north side. The hot water temperature of 138° can be controlled by adding river water. Bathing suits are advisable.

It is .5 miles to Troutdale Campground.

Directions: From Atlanta, drive west on FS 268 for about 35 miles. Look for a small rock pool on the near side of the river .7 miles after crossing a bridge over the river. Parking turnout is not available, but the road is wide here and traffic light.

Map Source: USGS *Sheep Creek* (pools on north side only).

472   SHEEP CREEK BRIDGE HOT SPRINGS
(see map on page 126)
● **Southwest of the town of Atlanta**

Shallow rock pool dug into a hillside several feet above the Middle Fork Boise River. Elevation 3,400 feet. Open all year.

Natural mineral water flows in a weak trickle down the hillside to a shallow rock pool laden with algae. The 142°-water cools as it flows down the hillside, and air contributes to the rest of the cooling. Bathing suits advised.

It is 2.5 miles to Troutdale Campground.

Directions: From Atlanta, travel 38 miles to a bridge where the road recrosses the river. Park in a small turnout at the east end of the bridge. The spring is located several feet above the river, 50 yards downstream from the bridge.

476 SAWTOOTH LODGE

(208) 259-3331

■ Grandjean, ID 83637

Historic, mountain resort in the Sawtooth Recreation Area. Elevation 5,100. Open June through October.

Natural mineral water flows out of several springs with temperatures up to 150° and into an outdoor, chlorinated swimming pool maintained at approximately 80°. The pool is available to the public as well as to registered guests. Bathing suits are required.

Dressing rooms, cafe, cabins, overnight camping, and RV hookups are available on the premises. It is 42 miles to a store and service station in Stanley. Visa and MasterCard are accepted.

Directions: From the town of Lowman, go 22 miles east on ID 21, then follow signs six miles on gravel road to the lodge.

477 SACAJAWEA HOT SPRINGS

● West of the town of Grandjean

Popular, large geothermal area on the north bank of the South Fork of the Payette River in Boise National Forest. Elevation 5,000 feet. Open all year.

Natural mineral water flows out of many springs at temperatures up to 108° and cools as it cascades into a series of volunteer-built rock pools along the river's edge. Because the pools are visible from the road, bathing suits are advisable.

There are no services available on the premises. It is one mile to a cafe, cabins, overnight camping, and RV hookups and 40 miles to a store and service station in Stanley.

Directions: From Lowman, drive 21 miles east on ID 21 to Grandjean turnoff (FS 524) on the right. Follow the gravel road 4.6 miles to Wapiti Creek Bridge. Look for springs on the right side of read, .6 miles past the bridge.

478   BONNEVILLE HOT SPRINGS

● **West of the town of Grandjean**

Popular, semi-remote geothermal area on a tree-lined creek in Boise National Forest. Elevation 4,800 feet. Open all year.

Natural mineral water flows out of a multitude of springs with various temperatures up to 180°. Be careful not to step into any of the scalding runoff channels. There is one small, wooden bathhouse with an individual tub supplied with water from a nearby spring at a temperature of 103°. Soakers drain the tub after each use. There are also many volunteer-built, rock-and-sand soaking pools along the edge of the creek where the geothermal water can be mixed with cold water. Bathing suits are advisable.

An adjacent campground with toilets is available for a fee. It is eight miles to a cafe, cabins, and RV hookups and 40 miles to a store and service station in Stanley.

Directions: From Lowman, drive 19 miles northeast to Bonneville Campground (formerly Warm Springs Campground). From the north edge of the campground, follow the unmarked but well-worn path .25 miles to the geothermal area.

479   KIRKHAM HOT SPRINGS

● **East of the town of Lowman**

Popular geothermal area with many hot waterfalls and pools adjoining a National Forest campground on the South Fork of the Payette River. Elevation 4,200 feet. Open all year.

Natural mineral water flows out of many springs and fissures along the south bank of the river at temperatures up to 120° and cools as it cascades toward the river. Volunteers have built several rock-and-sand soaking pools in which temperatures can vary above or below 100° depending on air temperature and wind conditions. Bathing suits are advisable, especially in the daytime.

Overnight camping is available in the adjoining campground. It is 38 miles to a cafe, store, service station, and cabins and 34 miles to RV hookups, all located near Stanley.

Directions: From the town of Lowman, go four miles east on ID 21 and watch for the Kirkham Hot Springs Campground sign.

Source map: *Boise National Forest*.

480   PINE FLATS HOT SPRING

● **West of the town of Lowman**

Spectacular, geothermal cascade and cliffside soaking pool overlooking the South Fork of the Payette River in Boise National Forest. Elevation 4,100 feet. Open all year.

Natural mineral water with temperatures up to 125° flows from several springs on top of a 100-foot-high cliff, cooling as it spills and tumbles over the rocks. There is one volunteer-built, tarp-lined rock pool 30 feet above the river, immediately below a hot shower-bath that averages 104°. Other rock pools at the foot of the cliff have lower temperatures. The apparent local custom is clothing optional.

The hot springs are located .33 miles from the Pine Flats Campground and parking area. It is 38 miles to a cafe, store, service station, and motel and 27 miles to RV hookups, all near the town of Stanley.

Directions: From the west edge of Pine Flats campground, follow an unmarked but well-worn path .33 miles west down to and along a large riverbed and rock-and-sand bar. Look for geothermal water cascading down the cliff onto the bar.

Source map: *Boise National Forest.*

It's amazing how many people camping here at this campground don't know of the existence of the lower soaking pools, let alone the fabulous hot water shower.

482   DEER CREEK HOT SPRINGS

● **West of the town of Crouch**

Small, volunteer-built soaking pool in a gully 20 yards from a paved highway, combining the flow from several springs, a test well, and a creek. Elevation 3,000 feet. Open all year.

Natural mineral water flows out of multiple springs and an abandoned well casing at temperatures ranging up to 176°. Volunteers have built a shallow, plastic-and-sand soaking pool on one side of the South Fork Payette River to mix the hot and cold water. There are no posted clothing requirements, but the proximity to the highway makes bathing suits advisable.

There are no services available on the premises, but all services are available four miles away.

Directions: From the town of Crouch, go 4.5 miles west toward the town of Banks, watching for a steep dirt road on the north side of the highway. Do not drive up the road; it dead ends in just a few yards. Park in a turnout on the river side of the highway and walk back to the springs, which are just below the steep side road.

Source map: *Boise National Forest.*

481   HOT SPRINGS CAMPGROUND

● **East of the town of Crouch**

The cement foundations of a long-gone bathhouse and some small, volunteer-built soaking pools are intended to use some of the continuing hot-water flow. Located on a riverbank across the highway from a National Forest campground. Elevation 3,800 feet. Open all year.

Natural mineral water flows out of several springs at 105° and into volunteer-built, shallow, rock-and-sand pools near the south side of the highway. Bathing suits are advisable.

Overnight camping is available on the premises. All other services are available four miles away.

Directions: From the town of Crouch, go four miles east toward Lowman. Look for Hot Springs Campground one mile after entering Forest Service land.

Source map: *Boise National Forest.*

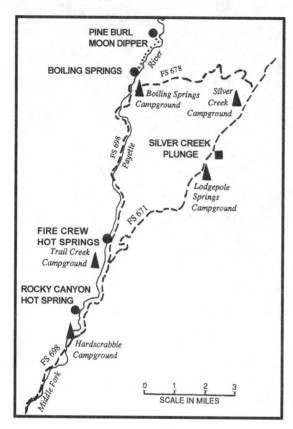

PINE BURL
MOON DIPPER

BOILING SPRINGS

FS 678

River

Boiling Springs
Campground

Silver
Creek
Campground

FS 698
Payette

SILVER CREEK
PLUNGE

Lodgepole
Springs
Campground

FS 671

FIRE CREW
HOT SPRINGS
Trail Creek
Campground

ROCKY CANYON
HOT SPRING

FS 698

Hardscrabble
Campground

Middle Fork

0   1   2   3
SCALE IN MILES

484   FIRE CREW HOT SPRINGS
(see map)

•   **North of the town of Crouch**

Several pools in a winding river canyon at the edge of the Middle Fork of the Payette River in Boise National Forest. Elevation 3,800 feet. Open all year.

Natural mineral water flows from springs at temperatures above 120° into a 15-foot, rock-edged pool adjacent to the river. By moving the rocks, cold river water can be added to the pool to adjust the temperature. The apparent local custom is clothing optional.

It is .5 miles to Trail Creek Campground and 15 miles to Crouch for all other services.

Directions: From Crouch, drive north on FS 698 toward Boiling Springs. About .3 miles past the junction with FS 671, look for a dirt road on the river side of FS 698. Follow the road for a short distance to a turnaround and parking area. The pools are located on the upstream end of the parking area.

483   ROCKY CANYON (ROBERTS) HOT SPRING
(see map)

•   **North of the town of Crouch**

Primitive hot spring on the Middle Fork of the Payette River in Boise National Forest. Elevation 4,000 feet. Open all year.

Natural mineral water flows out of a spring at 120°, then down a steep slope toward the river. To reach the spring, you must ford the river, which might not be safe during high water. Volunteers have built a series of primitive rock pools, each colder than the one above. All pools are visible from the road, so bathing suits are advisable.

There are no services available on the premises. It is 1.5 miles to Hardscrabble Campground, and 10 miles to all other services in Crouch.

Directions: From Crouch, take FS 698 about 12.5 miles and park in a turnout on your left. Pools are across the river, and fording the river should only be done in late summer or early fall.

Source map: *Boise National Forest.*

Silver Creek Plunge is one of the more remote resorts in an area surrounded by natural hot springs.

---

485   SILVER CREEK PLUNGE
(208) 344-8688 (unit 1942)
H/C 76 Box 237
(see map on facing page)
■   **Garden Valley, ID 83622**

Remote, mountain resort surrounded by Boise National Forest. Elevation 4,600 feet. Open all year; snowmobile access in winter.

Natural mineral water flows out of a spring at 101° directly into an outdoor swimming pool that is maintained at 84°. The pool operates on a flow-through basis, so it requires a minimum of chlorination. It is available to the public as well as to registered guests. Bathing suits are required.

Dressing rooms, snack bar, cabins, and overnight camping are available on the premises. It is 22 miles to a store, service station, and RV hookups. No credit cards are accepted.

Directions: From the town of Crouch, go north 14 miles on FS 698, then bear northeast on FS 671 for nine miles to the plunge.

Source map: *Boise National Forest*.

486   BOILING SPRINGS
(see map on facing page)

●   **North of the town of Crouch**

Large, geothermal water flow on the Middle Fork of the Payette River in Boise National Forest. Elevation 4,200 feet. Open all year.

Natural mineral water flows out of a cliff at more than 130° into a pond adjacent to the Boiling Springs guard station. The water cools as it flows through a ditch to join the river. Summer volunteers usually build a rock-and-mud dam at the point where the water is cool enough for soaking or where river water can be added. Because of the nearby campground, bathing suits are advisable.

No services are available on the premises. It is .25 miles to Boiling Springs Campground and 19 miles to all other services in Crouch.

Directions: From the north edge of Boiling Springs Campground, follow the path .25 miles to the guard station and spring.

Source map: *Boise National Forest*.

Moon Dipper Hot Spring (left) offers a view down the canyon and down Dash Creek, while *Pine Burl Hot Spring* has enough room for a cozy couple or for a single person to meditate quietly in the peacefulness of nature.

487A MOON DIPPER HOT SPRING AND
487B PINE BURL HOT SPRING
(see map on page 138)

● **North of the town of Crouch**

Two lovely, remote and primitive hot springs on the bank of Dash Creek, very close together in Boise National Forest. Elevation 4,200 feet. Open all year.

Natural mineral water flows out of two springs at 120° and directly into volunteer-built, rock soaking pools. Water temperature in the pools is controlled by mixing cold creek water with the hot water. Moon Dipper, a large, sandy-bottom pool, has a nice canyon view, while Pine Burl offers a small, romantic spot for two. The apparent local custom is clothing optional.

No services are available on the premises. It is a two-mile hike to overnight camping and 21 miles to all other services.

Directions: From the Boiling Springs guard station, follow a well-used (sometimes slippery) but unmarked path along the river for a two-mile hike to the springs.

Source maps: *Boise National Forest*; USGS *Boiling Springs, Idaho* (springs not on quad).

Note: There are several more primitive hot springs with the potential for volunteer-built soaking pools further upstream from Moon Dipper and Pine Burl. However, all of them require that the river be forded many times with a high risk of losing the faint, unmarked path. Consult a Boise National Forest ranger before attempting to hike to any of these springs.

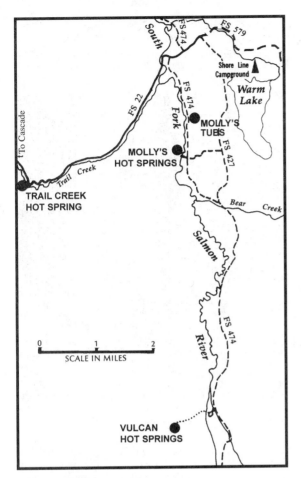

488   TRAIL CREEK (BREIT) HOT SPRING
(see map)

● **West of Warm Lake**

Small, beautiful hot spring, soaking pool, and bathtub in a narrow canyon down a steep, 60-yard path from a paved highway in Boise National Forest. Elevation 6,000 feet. Open all year.

Natural mineral water flows out of a fissure in the rocks adjoining Trail Creek at 125°. Volunteers have placed a white enamel bathtub in the creekbed and installed a hose to bring in this hot water. Bring a bucket with which to add cold creek water when desired. Volunteers have also built a primitive, rock-and-sand soaking pool on the edge of the creek where the temperature can be controlled by changing the amount of cold creek water admitted. You may have to rebuild this pool if you are the first ones in, as high water tends to wash it out every year. The apparent local custom is clothing optional.

No services are available on the premises. It is two miles to a campground, seven miles to gas, cafe, cabins, and phone at Warm Lake Lodge (open Memorial Day to October 15), and 22 miles to all other services in Cascade.

Directions: from the intersection of FS 22 and FS 474 west of Warm Lake, go west 3.7 miles and look for an especially large parking area on the south side of the road. From the west edge of this parking area, the pool is visible at the bottom of Trail Creek canyon. There is no maintained trail, so be careful scrambling down the steep path.

Source map: *Boise National Forest*.

There are only a few places which give you a choice of a bathtub or a natural pool at the creek's edge—either one is great fun at *Trail Creek Hot Spring*.

489A   MOLLY'S HOT SPRING
(see map on page 141)

- **West of Warm Lake**

A tarp-lined pool on the side of a steep, geothermal hillside overlooking the South Fork of the Salmon River in Boise National Forest. Locals named this one "the Duke" in honor of repeated visits from John Wayne and Robert Mitchum. Elevation 5,400 feet. Open all year.

Natural mineral water flows out of several springs at temperatures up to 120° and is transported downhill by a variety of pipes and hoses. Water temperature in the volunteer-built pool is controlled by diverting or combining the hotter and cooler flows. Additional volunteer work could produce an excellent chest-deep pool. The apparent local custom is clothing optional.

No services are available on the premises. It is three miles to overnight camping, five miles to gas, cafe, store, cabins, and phone at Warm Lake Lodge (open Memorial Day to October 15), and 25 miles to all other services in Cascade.

Directions: From the intersection of FS 22 (paved) and FS 474 (gravel), go 1.7 miles south on FS 474 to the intersection with a road where a sign directs you east to Warm Lake. The road leading west from this intersection has been blocked to vehicle traffic, but it is passable on foot. Park and walk west on this blocked road 300 yards, cross the old bridge, and immediately turn right onto a trail that is just above the fallen trees at the waters edge. Follow the trail 100 yards north to the thermal area.

Source map: *Boise National Forest.*

489B MOLLY'S TUBS
(see map on page 141)

● **West of Warm Lake**

A much-used collection of bathtubs on the South Fork of the Salmon River in Boise National Forest. Elevation 5,200 feet. Open all year.

Natural mineral water flows out of several springs at approximately 120° and is piped through hoses to eight bathtubs. Buckets are used for adding cold water from the nearby river. The tubs are lined up in two groups so you can have relative privacy if desired. Take a roll of duct tape for sealing leaks and drain holes. The apparent local custom is clothing optional.

There are no services available on the premises. It is 1.5 miles to a campground, 3.5 miles to Warm Lake Lodge (open Memorial Day to October 15), and 24 miles to all other services in Cascade.

Directions: From the intersection of FS 22 (paved) and FS 474 (gravel), go 1.3 miles south on FS 474 to a pullout on right. Follow a steep path down to the tubs.

Source map: *Boise National Forest*.

490　VULCAN HOT SPRINGS
(see map on page 147)

● **South of Warm Lake**

Still popular, geothermal creek pools in the Boise National Forest which seem to be getting hotter each year. The trees, once insect-ravaged, seem to be making some degree of comeback. Elevation 5,600 feet. Open all year.

Natural mineral water flows out of many small, bubbling springs at boiling temperatures, creating a substantial hot creek that gradually cools as it runs through the woods toward the South Fork of the Salmon River. Volunteers have built a log dam across this creek at the point where the water has cooled to approximately 105+° (depending on air and water temperature). This dam has been partly wiped out by high-water runoff, and the one-mile trail to it is no longer maintained. The apparent local custom is clothing optional.

One mile south of Stole Meadows there is an unmarked, unofficial camping area where the head of the trail to the springs begins. It is seven miles to a Forest Service campground and 32 miles to all other services.

Directions: At the west edge of the camping area is a log footbridge built by the Corps of Engineers. Cross this bridge and follow the path across two more log bridges. It is approximately one mile to the dam and pool.

Source maps: *Boise National Forest*; USGS *Warm Lake, Idaho*.

491 SUGAH (MILE 16) HOT SPRING

● **North of Warm Lake**

A sweetie of a remote soaking pool for two, located on the edge of the South Fork of the Salmon River in Payette National Forest. Elevation 4,800 feet. Open all year.

Natural mineral water flows out of a spring at 115° and cools as it goes through makeshift pipes to the volunteer-built, rock-and-masonry pool at the river's edge. Pool temperature is controlled by diverting the hot water and/or by adding a bucket of cold river water. The apparent local custom is clothing optional.

There are no services available on the premises. There is a campground within two miles, and it is 40 miles to all other services.

Directions: From the intersection of FS 22 (paved) and FS 474 (gravel), go north on FS 474 along the South Fork of the Salmon River for 16 miles to the spring. At 1.7 miles past Poverty Flats Campground, there is a small (two-car) turnout on the side of the road toward the river. Look for an unmarked, steep path down to the pool.

Note: Due to forest fires this pool has been inaccessible for the last two to three seasons, although word has it that FS 474 is now being paved.

Source maps: *Payette National Forest; Boise National Forest*.

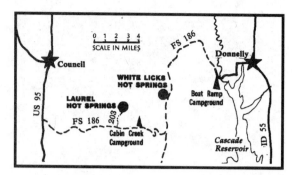

492   WHITE LICKS HOT SPRINGS
(see map)

- **West of the Donnelly**

A large, geothermal seep serving two small bath-houses in an unofficial camping area at a wooded site surrounded by Payette National Forest. Elevation 4,800 feet. Open all year.

Natural mineral water flows out of many small springs at temperatures up to 120°, supplying two small, wood shacks, each containing a cement tub. Each tub is served by two pipes, one bringing in 110° water, the other bringing in 80° water. The tub temperature is controlled by plugging up the pipe bringing in the water not desired. Soakers are expected to drain the tub after each use. Bathing suits are not required inside the bathhouses.

A picnic area and camping are available on the premises. It is 16 miles to all other services.

Directions: From ID 55 in Donnelly, follow signs west toward Rainbow Point Campground. After crossing the bridge across Cascade Reservoir, follow FS 186 (gravel) as it starts north, curves west, and then goes south. Watch for the hot spring on the west side of FS 186, 3.5 miles south of the intersection of FS 245 and FS 186.

It tickles when the hot water comes up through the creekbed and surrounds you in the several pools down the middle of the creek at *Laurel Hot Springs*.

493   LAUREL HOT SPRINGS
(see map)

- **East of the town of Council**

Several primitive, thermal springs in a wooded canyon at the end of a rugged, two-mile hike in Payette National Forest. Elevation 4,300 feet. Open all year.

Natural mineral water flows out of several springs at temperatures up to 120° and into progressively cooler, volunteer-built soaking pools along the bottom of Warm Springs Creek. The local custom is clothing optional.

There are no services available on the premises. It is two miles to a campground and 23 miles to all other services.

Directions: From Cabin Creek Campground on FS 186, go two miles west to Warm Springs Creek. Follow trail number 203 two miles north to the springs. Water is very hot where the trail crosses the creek.

Source map: *Payette National Forest.*

494 WATERHOLE LODGE
PO Box 37   (208) 634-7758
☐   Lake Fork, ID 83635

Remodeled tavern, lodge, and unique hot tubs with a view of the mountains. Located five miles south of McCall.

Private-space hot pools using bromine-treated tap water are for rent to the public by the hour. There are six redwood hydrojet tubs in covered patios with one side that opens on a mountain view. Pool temperatures range from 102-106°. Each unit has an inside, heated dressing room.

A cafe, tavern, rooms, and overnight camping are available on the premises. A store and service station are within five blocks, and RV hookups are within five miles. Visa and MasterCard are accepted. Phone for rates, reservations, and directions.

495 KRIGBAUM HOT SPRINGS

●   **East of the town of Meadows**

Primitive hot springs and soaking pool on the east bank of Goose Creek, surrounded by Payette National Forest. Elevation 4,000 feet. Open all year.

Natural mineral water flows out of a spring at 102° and is piped to a volunteer-built, rock-and-cement pool where the temperatures range from 85-95°, depending on weather conditions. The apparent local custom is clothing optional.

There are no services available on the premises. It is two miles to a store, service station, overnight camping, and RV hookups and nine miles to a motel and restaurant.

Directions: On ID 55, go one mile east from Packer Johns Cabin State Park and turn north on the gravel road along the east bank of Goose Creek. Just before the road crosses a bridge over Goose Creek, park and hike 300 yards north along the east bank to the pool.

Source map: *Payette National Forest.*

496   ZIM'S HOT SPRINGS
PO Box 314   (208) 347-9447
New Meadows, ID 83654

Older, rural plunge and picnic grounds in an agricultural valley. Elevation 4,200 feet. Open all year.

Natural mineral water flows out of an artesian well at 151° and is cooled as it is sprayed into the chlorine-treated pools. The temperature in the outdoor swimming pool ranges from 90-100° and from 103-106° in the outdoor soaking pool. Bathing suits are required.

Locker rooms, snacks, picnic area, overnight camping, and RV hookups are available on the premises. A store, service station, and motel are located within four miles. Visa and MasterCard are accepted.

Directions: From the town of New Meadows, take US 95 four miles north, then follow signs to the plunge.

497   THE LODGE AT RIGGINS HOT SPRINGS
PO Box 1247   (208) 628-3785
Riggins, ID 83549

Secluded 155-acre luxury resort on the banks of the Salmon River, 10 miles east of Riggins. Elevation 1,800 feet. Open all year.

Natural mineral water flows out of an artesian well at 140° and is piped to the recently remodeled soaking pool and enclosed spa. Water temperature in the flow-though spa is maintained at 105-108° without chlorination. Water temperature in the flow-through pool is maintained at 92-97° with a minimum of chlorination. The pools are open only to registered guests. Bathing suits are required.

Rooms with private baths are available in the main lodge and in a new three unit cabin. A stocked trout pond, a bathhouse with game room, and access to the Salmon River are available on the premises. Whitewater rafting, steelhead fishing, jet-boat excursions, and horses are available nearby. Visa and MasterCard are accepted.

Phone for rates, reservations, and directions.

498   BURGDORF HOT SPRINGS

■ **McCall, ID 83638**

Picturesque, mountain-rustic resort without electricity or telephone, surrounded by Payette National Forest. Elevation 6,000 feet. Open all year.

Natural mineral water flows out of a spring at 112° and directly into and through a sandy-bottom swimming pool that averages 100° and requires no chemical treatment. The pools are available only to registered guests. Bathing suits are required during the daytime.

Dressing rooms and cabins with outdoor plumbing are available on the premises.

Overnight camping is within .25 miles. It is 30 miles to all other services. Hiking, skiing, snowmobiling, and boating are nearby. No credit cards are accepted.

Write first for reservations and information on current status and what to bring. For wintertime pickup by snowmobile, write to the resort managers, Richard and Elizabeth Tidmarsh, General Delivery, McCall, ID 83638.

MONTANA

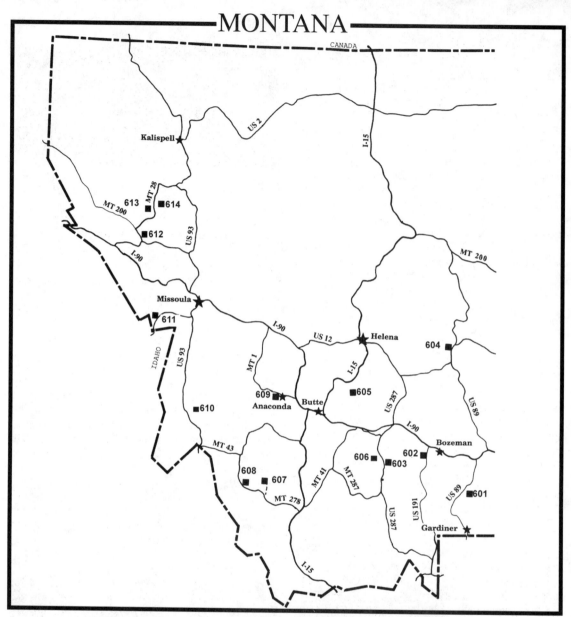

CANADA

Kalispell ★

US 2

I-15

MT 28
613 ■ ■614
MT 200 ■612
US 93
I-90

MT 200

Missoula ★
■ 611

IDAHO
US 93

I-90
US 12
Helena ★
■ 604

MT 1
I-15

609 ■★
Anaconda Butte ★
■605
US 287

■610

US 89

MT 43
608 ■ ■ 607

MT 41
MT 287

606 ■ ■
■603
602 ■
Bozeman ★
I-90

US 89
■601

MT 278

US 287
US 191

Gardiner ★

I-15

This map was designed to be used with a standard highway map.

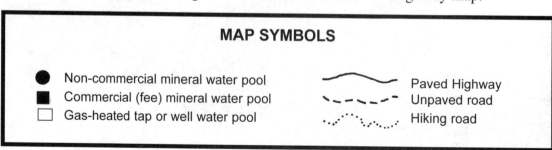

MAP SYMBOLS

● Non-commercial mineral water pool
■ Commercial (fee) mineral water pool
□ Gas-heated tap or well water pool

〜 Paved Highway
- - - Unpaved road
····· Hiking road

601 CHICO HOT SPRINGS
PO Box 127 (406) 333-4933
Pray, MT 59065

Large, year-round resort established in 1900, surrounded by Gallatin National Forest. Elevation 5,000 feet. Open all year.

Natural mineral water flows out of several springs at 118° and is piped into a nearly Olympic-size, open-air pool maintained at 98°. The adjacent covered soaking pool is kept at 105°. One private-space hot tub, rented separately, is held at 105°. All pools operate on a flow-through basis. Pools are available to the public as well as to resort guests. Bathing suits are required.

Accommodations are available in the Main Lodge and in two motels, log cabins, and condominiums. The resort offers dining in the Chico Inn and Poolside Grille, a saloon with live entertainment on weekends. Horseback riding, mountain bike rentals, dogsled treks, and summer raft trips are also available. It is three miles to a store with a gas pump and three miles to a full-service campground. Visa, Discover, and MasterCard are accepted.

Directions: Located approximately 24 miles south of Livingston. From the town of Emigrant on US 89, turn southeast on Murphy Lane (SR 362) .8 miles to stop sign, then left on SR 540. Go .5 miles, then first right onto the Chico Road (SR 542). Resort is 1.5 miles up the road, 31 miles north of Gardner.

602 BOZEMAN HOT SPRINGS
81123 Gallatin Rd. (406) 587-3030
Bozeman, MT 59715

Tree-shaded KOA campground with mineral water pools. Elevation 4,500 feet. Open all year. Pools closed from sundown Friday to sundown Saturday.

Natural mineral water flows out of a spring at 141° and is piped to an indoor pool building. The swimming pool is maintained at 90°, and adjoining soaking pools are maintained at temperatures ranging from 100-110°. There is also a 60° cold pool. All pools operate on a flow-through basis, including the cold tap water for controlling temperatures. Minimal chemical treatment is required. Pools are available to the public as well as to registered guests. Bathing suits are required.

Locker rooms, grocery store, laundromat, picnic area, RV hookups, and Kamper Kabins are available on the premises. It is one mile to a restaurant and service station and eight miles to a motel. Visa and MasterCard are accepted.

Location: On US 191, eight miles southwest of the town of Bozeman.

Bozeman Hot Springs offers several different pools with varying temperatures for everyone to enjoy.

603   BEAR TRAP HOT SPRINGS
PO Box 2944   (406) 685-3303
■❖   Norris, MT 59745

Small RV park in foothills below Tobacco Root Mountains. Elevation 5,000 feet. Open all year.

Natural mineral water flows out of artesian springs at 128°. The outdoor soaking pool is maintained at 101° in the summer and 106° in the winter. The water contains no sulfur, and only minimal chemical treatment is necessary because the pool operates on a flow-through basis. The pool is available to the public as well as to registered guests. Bathing suits are required.

A store, picnic area, overnight camping and RV hookups are available on the premises. It is .25 miles to a cafe and service station and 10 miles to a motel. No credit cards are accepted.

Directions: From US 287 in the town of Norris, go .25 miles east on MT 84.

604   SPA MOTEL
PO Box 370   (406) 225-4339
■   White Sulphur Springs, MT 59645

Remodeled, older resort at the foot of the Castle Mountains. Elevation 5,100. Open all year.

Natural mineral water flows out of a spring at 120° and is piped to two pools that operate on a flow-through basis, requiring no chemical treatment. The outdoor swimming pool is maintained at 94° in the summer and 102° in the winter. The indoor soaking pool is maintained at 106-108°. Bathing suits are required.

Rooms and a picnic area are available on the premises. It is less that five blocks to all other services. Visa and MasterCard are accepted.

Location: On US 89 at the west end of White Sulphur Springs.

Bear Trap Hot Springs: This artesian spring operates 24 hours a day offering a refreshing shower to go along with your soak.

Boulder Hot Springs: Originally designated as a sanctuary by the Native Americans and consequently called Peace Valley, the hot springs lies at the edge of Deerlodge National Forest, home to bear, moose, deer, fox, antelope, and coyote. Renovations continue to be made to this 100-year-old grand hotel.

605   BOULDER HOT SPRINGS
PO Box 930   (406) 225-4339
■   Boulder, MT 59632

Large historic resort built in 1888 is carefully being restored to its former charm. Nestled in the heart of Montana's Peace Valley, it was the first permanent building in the area. It is on 274 acres at the edge of Deerlodge National Forest and was designated by the Indians as a sanctuary where fighting was not permitted. Elevation 5,000 feet. Open all year. Pools are available on a day-use basis during the summer. Call about off-season hours.

Natural mineral water, pure enough to drink, flows out of several springs at temperatures between 150° and 175° and is piped to indoor and outdoor pools where it is cooled with water from the cold spring. Three newly tiled indoor pools with changing and shower area, offer men and women separate facilities for soaking. The women's bathhouse offers one hot pool maintained at 104° and a cooler one at 70°, while the men's bathhouse has one hot pool at 104°. All indoor plunges are large enough for at least 30 people. Water continually flows through every four hours, and all pools are completely drained and filled nightly. There are saunas in both bathhouses, and bathing suits are optional.

The outdoor swimming pool is treated with chlorine, and water temperatures ranging from 92-95°, depending on season. Bathing suits are required. All pools are handicap accessible with assistance.

Overnight accommodations, including meals, are offered to groups of 15 or more for seminars, workshops, and retreats. There are guest rooms for up to 60 people. Breakfast is served daily. Seven rooms have been remodeled for bed and breakfast service. Several rooms are wheelchair accessible. There is ample level ground near the pond or trees for tent camping or self-contained RVs. Nearby attractions include plenty of hiking, skiing, fishing, panoramic views, Elkhorn Ghost Town, Lewis and Clark Caverns State Park, and the Radon Mines, known for their therapeutic qualities. Other services are available in nearby Boulder, Butte, or Helena. No pets or alcohol are allowed on the premises. Visa and MasterCard accepted.

Boulder Hot Springs is approximately midway between Helena and Butte on I-15. Airport pickup can be arranged. Phone for rates, reservations, and directions.

The swimming pool at *Potosi Hot Springs* is built right into the granite cliffs above Potosi Creek. The lodge was originally built in 1890.

Inside this private cabin is a Japanese-style soaking tub with views of the nearby peaks and Potosi Creek. Dinner for two can be ordered in advance.

606 POTOSI HOT SPRINGS
PO Box 651   (406) 685 3594
■ **Pony, MT 59747**

Newly constructed and well-equipped rustic log cabins and lodge on the site of an 1890s historic hotel originally built for gold miners of the area. Located in the Tobacco Root Mountains in Beaverhead National Forest. Elevation 7,000 feet. Open all year. Roads are kept plowed in winter.

Geothermal, sulfur-free mineral water flows up through the ground and emerges from granite cliffs directly into the large outdoor recreational pool where there is continual flow-through so that only minimal chlorination is necessary. The 20- by 60-foot pool is maintained at 84-85°. It is drained and scrubbed every two weeks, or more frequently if needed.

The Spring House, a private indoor soaking pool, enclosed by a Japanese-style insulated wooden hut, contains a rock pool that dates back to the 1890s. Water from a separate spring flows in by gravity at 90°, with a shut-off valve for draining and cleaning. Lanterns and candles are provided to complement the private dinners that can be ordered ahead. During the day sunlight streams in through a picturesque window.

Part of the runoff from the pools goes into the creek; and part is channeled through pipes into the lodge and cabins for heating. Spring water is used for drinking and showers. Pools are handicap accessible, with assistance. Management has an open policy about bathing suit requirements, leaving it up to the consensus of the bathers. Pools and facilities are available to registered guests only.

Facilities include a changing room near the pools, a lodge, and creek-front cabins that sleep up to six. One cabin is wheelchair accessible. Breakfast is served daily in the lodge and included in the overnight price. Dinner is by pre-arranged reservations only. Tepees, sleeping up to six, are also available. Camping equipment is not included. Gas, grocery store, restaurant, and all other services are nine miles away in Harrison. Summer and winter outdoor activities are readily available on site and in the surrounding area. Reservations can be made through the resort. Visa, MasterCard, and personal checks are accepted.

Phone for rates, reservations, and directions.

Note: Reports are that there are some natural source pools in the vicinity. You might want to ask about them when you arrive.

607 ELKHORN HOT SPRINGS
PO Box 460514   (800) 722-8978
■   **Polaris, MT 59746**

Beautifully restored mountain resort, rustic lodge and cabins situated among the tall trees of Beaverhead National Forest. Elevation 7,300 feet. Open all year.

Natural mineral water flows out of six springs with temperatures ranging from 106-120°. The outdoor swimming pool is maintained at 88-95° and the outdoor soaking pool at 95-104°. There is one coed Roman sauna maintained at 105-108°. All pools are drained and refilled weekly. Pools are available to the public as well as to registered guests. Bathing suits are required.

Dressing rooms, restaurant, tent spaces, picnic area, overnight camping, and cabins are available on the premises. Horseback riding, backpacking, hunting, fishing, rock and mineral hunting, skiing, and snowmobile trails are available nearby. Cross-country ski rental is available on the premises. Pick-up service is provided from the city of Butte by prior arrangement. Visa and MasterCard are accepted.

Directions: Elkhorn Hot Springs is 43 miles northwest of Dillon, and 65 miles southwest of Butte. From I-15 three miles south of Dillon, take MT 278 west 27 miles to the large sign for Maverick Mt. Ski Area, Polaris, etc. Turn north and follow gravel road 13 miles to the resort.

Elkhorn Hot Springs invites you to enjoy both summer and winter sports in an atmosphere reminiscent of the Old West. The pools, of course, are an added plus.

Jackson Hot Springs was discovered by Lewis and Clark in 1806 and mentioned in Clark's journal. Jackson is surrounded by several mountain ranges with numerous streams and high mountain lakes. Wildlife, including golden and bald eagles, is abundant.

608   JACKSON HOT SPRINGS
PO Box 808   (406) 834-3151
■ **Jackson, MT 59736**

Renovated lodge and cabins on the main street of a small town. Log construction, knotty pine interiors, and a massive stone fireplace in the main lodge add to the rustic warmth and western charm. Elevation 6,400 feet. Open all year.

Natural mineral water flows out of a spring at 137° and is piped to cabins and a large 30- by 75-foot outdoor pool. The temperature in the pool is maintained at 98-100° and operates on a flow-through basis with only minimum chlorination. Water temperatures in cabin bathtubs can be controlled by adding cold tap water as needed. The swimming pool is available to the public as well as to registered guests. Bathing suits are required.

Facilities include dressing rooms, lodge complex with 16 cabins, a full-service restaurant, large western-style bar, and dance hall. Overnight camping and RV hookups are available on the premises. It is one block to a store and service station. Visa and MasterCard are accepted.

Location: On MT 278 on the main street in the town of Jackson.

609   FAIRMONT HOT SPRINGS
1500 Fairmont Rd.   (406) 797-3241
■ **Anaconda, MT 59711**

Large hotel-type resort and real-estate development in a wide valley. Elevation 5,300. Open all year.

Natural mineral water flows out of a spring at 160° and is piped to a 350-foot enclosed water slide and a group of pools, where it is treated with chlorine. The indoor and outdoor swimming pools are maintained at 80-85° and the indoor and outdoor soaking pools at 105°. There are also men's and women's steam rooms. Facilities are available to the public as well as to registered guests. Bathing suits are required.

Locker rooms, restaurant, lounge, rooms, mini-zoo, tennis, golf course, and horseback riding are available on the premises. Overnight camping, RV hookups, country store, and service station are one block away. Fishing, snowmobiling, hunting, and skiing are all close by. Visa, MasterCard, Discover, and American Express are accepted.

Directions: From I-90 12 miles west of Butte, take the Gregson-Fairmont exit (#211) and follow signs to the resort.

Fairmont Hot Springs: A 350-foot enclosed water slide, along with a mini-zoo, makes the Fairmont a popular destination resort for families with children. Adults can entertain themselves with golf, tennis, and horseback riding right on the premises.

Lost Trails Hot Springs Resort: Known in previous times as Gallogly Springs, this resort has a colorful history. For years it was a secluded stopping place for travelers crossing the Continental Divide at the pass. The old Indian trail climbs about 2,000 feet in three miles, making it a very difficult trek. People would often stop to rest at the springs before starting the long climb. Later, farmers taking their produce to market would stop at the springs for the night.

---

610 LOST TRAILS HOT SPRINGS RESORT

8221 Hwy 93 S	(406) 821-3574
■ Sula, MT 59871	(800) 825-3574

Historic rustic mountain resort, located on beautifully forested private land within the Bitterroot National Forest. Elevation 5,000 feet. Open all year. Call ahead in winter when pools may be closed Monday and Tuesday.

Natural mineral water bubbles up at 108-110° and flows by gravity through pipes at 100 gallons per minute to a large 21- by 70-foot outdoor swimming pool. Runoff is diverted to the creek below. Inflow pipes are laid under the concrete surrounding the pools so they don't ice up in winter. There is an adjoining 10-inch deep, 10- by 21-foot kiddy pool. The pools are covered by a dome in winter, keeping the air temperature warm enough to grow bananas or oranges.

Indoors is a sauna and a fiberglass hot tub in a separate wood-paneled room. The water temperature is maintained at 106°. Pools and sauna are available on a day-use basis.

Facilities include dressing rooms, rustic housekeeping cabins, a motel, two lodges which can accommodate large groups and family reunions of up to 30 people, full bar with casino, restaurant, fireplace, children's play area, and a convenience store. There are also RV spaces with hookups. A National Forest campground is .2 miles north of the resort.

Activities in the surrounding wilderness area include hiking, alpine and Nordic skiing, fishing, backpacking, horseback riding, and rafting. Snowmobiles and cross-country skis are available for rent at the resort. It is six miles to a post office/general store in Sula and 25 miles to all other services in Darby. Most major credit cards are accepted.

Location: On Hwy 93, 6 miles south of Sula, Montana, 6 miles north of the Montana-Idaho border at Lost Trails Pass. The resort is 88 miles south of Missoula, Montana and 55 miles north of Salmon, Idaho.

611   LOLO HOT SPRINGS RESORT
■   **38500 Highway 12   (406) 273-2290**
Lolo, MT 59847   (800) 273-2290

An historic resort that has been restored and expanded, nestled in the heart of the Lolo National Forest near the Selway-Bitterroot Wilderness, 30 miles west of Missoula. Elevation 4,700 feet. Open all year.

Natural mineral water flows out of two springs at temperatures of 110° and 117° and is piped to two pools that are built directly over the springs themselves. Water is pumped up into the pools, and with continual flow-through, the water in each pool is completely changed every 24 hours, requiring only minimal chlorination. The large outdoor pool maintains a temperature of 92-98°. The covered soaking pool maintains a temperature of 103-105°. Bathing suits are required.

Facilities include dressing rooms, bathhouse, RV park, campground, tepees for rent, and a picnic area. New full-service restaurant; saloon with casino, pool table, and dance floor; mini-gift shop, and newly built rustic log motel are available on the premises. Most facilities are open year-round. Recreational activities include hiking, mountain biking, horseback riding, snowmobiling, and cross-country skiing. Horse and snowmobile rental are available from the lodge. Call during heavy snow regarding status of RV park and campgrounds. Visa and MasterCard are accepted. All other services are available 25 miles east in Lolo. Phone for rates and reservations.

Location: On US 12, 25 miles west of Lolo, MT, seven miles east of the Montana-Idaho border.

Quinn's Paradise Resort: Fun is the key word for this family resort where kids and their parents can soak in the separate outdoor swimming and hydrojet pools.

612   QUINN'S PARADISE RESORT:
A NATURAL HOT SPRINGS
■   **PO Box 219   (406) 826-3150**
Paradise, MT 59856

Complete family resort on the banks of the Clark Fork River. Elevation 2,700 feet. Open all year.

Natural mineral water flows out of a spring at 120°. The outdoor swimming pool is treated with chlorine and maintained at a temperature of 88°. The outdoor hydrojet pool is maintained at 100° and operates on a flow-through basis so that only minimal chemical treatment of the water is needed. There are two indoor, private-space fiberglass tubs in which the water temperature can be controlled by the customer. These pools are drained and refilled after each use, so that no chemical treatment is necessary. Pools are available to the public as well as to registered guests. Bathing suits are required except in private spaces.

Dressing rooms, cafe, bar, store, rooms and cabins, overnight camping, RV hookups, and fishing are available on the premises. It is 11 miles to the service station in Plains (on MT 200). Most major credit cards are accepted.

Location: On MT 135, three miles south of the junction with MT 200, which is east of St. Regis.

613 SYMES HOTEL AND MEDICINAL SPRINGS

(406) 741-2361

■ **Hot Springs, MT 59845**

Historic hotel with a long tradition of mineral water and other health treatments. Elevation 2,900 feet. Open all year.

Natural mineral water flows out of an artesian well at 80-90° and is heated as needed for use in soaking tubs. There are nine individual soaking tubs in the men's bathhouse and six in the women's bathhouse. There are also hotel rooms with mineral water piped to the room. Temperature is controllable within each tub, and no chemical treatment is added. Bathhouses are available to the public as well as to registered guests.

Locker rooms, hotel rooms, and chiropractic services are available on the premises. It is two blocks to a cafe, store, and service station and six blocks to overnight camping and RV hookups. No credit cards are accepted.

Directions: From MT 382 northeast of St. Regis, follow signs to the town of Hot Springs and then to the hotel.

614 WILD HORSE HOT SPRINGS

PO Box K   (406) 741-3777

■ **Hot Springs, MT 59845**

Well-maintained, family rent-a-tub establishment with overnight facilities surrounded by rolling foothills. Elevation 2,750 feet. Open all year.

Natural mineral water flows out of an artesian well at 124° and is piped to the bathhouse building. There are six large indoor soaking pools in private rooms, each with steam bath, sauna, shower, and toilet. Pool water temperature is controllable by each customer up to 110°. The pools are scrubbed down frequently, so no chemical treatment is needed. Bathing suits are not required in private rooms. Geothermal heat is used in all buildings.

Cabins, picnic area, overnight camping, and RV hookups are available on the premises. It is six miles to all other services. No credit cards are accepted.

Directions: From MT 28, 2.5 miles north of Hot Springs junction, follow signs two miles east on the gravel road to the resort.

WYOMING

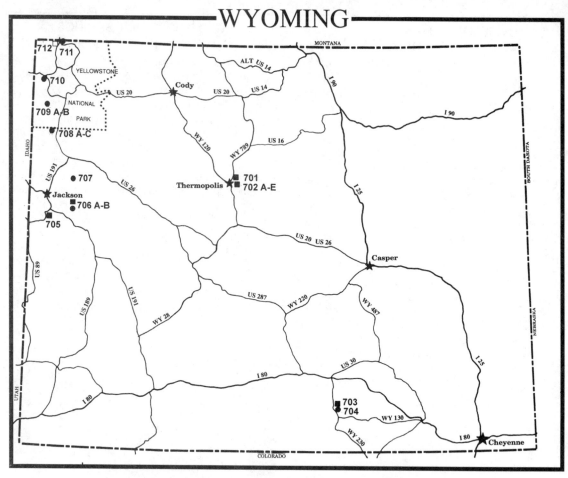

This map was designed to be used with a standard highway map.

MAP SYMBOLS

● Non-commercial mineral water pool
■ Commercial (fee) mineral water pool
□ Gas-heated tap or well water pool

〜 Paved Highway
- - - Unpaved road
⋯ Hiking road

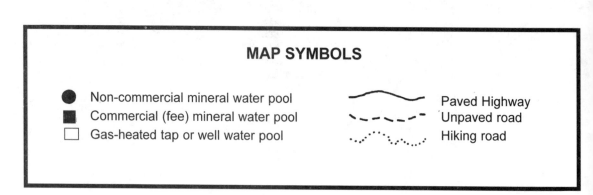

701   FOUNTAIN OF YOUTH RV PARK
PO Box 711   (307) 864-3265
■   **Thermopolis, WY 82443**

Well-kept RV park featuring a unique, large soaking pool. Elevation 4,300 feet. Open March 1 to October 31.

Natural mineral water flows out of the historic Sacajawea Well at the rate of over one million gallons per day. Some of this 130° water is channeled through a cooling pond into a 200-foot-long soaking pool where the temperature varies from 104° at the inflow end to 99° at the outflow. A special ramp makes the pool handicap accessible. The pool is available only to registered day and overnight campers. Bathing suits are required.

Rest rooms, showers, picnic sites, laundry, RV supplies, overnight camping, and RV hookups are available on the premises. It is two miles to all other services. Visa and MasterCard are accepted.

Location: On US 20, two miles north of the town of Thermopolis.

These families are enjoying the largest mineral pool in Wyoming and the third largest in the world.

It is probable that the well that fills this 235-foot by 72-foot pool taps the same hot mineral water reservoir as that which supplies the Big Spring in Thermopolis. The water flow is so enormous that the pool water is exchanged every 11 hours. The well was originally drilled in 1918 in a search for oil. Instead, hot mineral water came gushing out under such pressure that the derrick was destroyed.

Thermopolis, a Greek word for "Hot City," is located next to Hot Springs State Park, which offers several different places to enjoy a hot mineral soak. All of the establishments on the grounds are supplied with natural mineral water from the Big Springs. Big Horn Hot Springs releases 2.8 million gallons daily and is one of the largest mineral springs in the world.

Walkways have been provided through the large tufa terraces that have been built up by mineral deposits from the spring over the centuries. These terraces, hot waterfalls, and the state's bison herd—in addition to a nice relaxing soak—makes the trip to the park, which is only two hours from Yosemite, well worthwhile.

This square mile of land was presented to the State of Wyoming by the Federal Government after it had been purchased from the Shoshone and Arapahoe Indians in 1896. Annually, in August, the Shoshone Indians set up their tepees and reenact the "Wedding of the Waters," portraying the sale of the springs.

For more information, contact Hot Springs Water Park, (307) 864-9250.

702A   HOT SPRINGS WATER PARK

PO Box 750   (307) 864-9250
■ Thermopolis, WY 82443

The outdoor and indoor swimming pools are maintained at 85-95° year-round, and the indoor soaking pool is maintained at 104°. The indoor steambath is maintained at 110-115°. There are three outdoor hot tubs with temperatures varying from 100-104° and indoor/outdoor water slides. All pools operate on a flow-through basis, so only minimal chemical treatment is needed. Bathing suits are required.

Locker rooms and a snack bar are available on the premises. Visa and MasterCard are accepted.

702B   STATE BATH HOUSE

State Park   (307) 864-3765
■ Thermopolis, WY 82443

The outdoor and indoor soaking pools are maintained at 104°. The temperature in 16 (eight men's and eight women's) individual soaking tubs is adjustable by the person using the tub. All pools use minimally chlorinated, flow-through mineral water. No charge is made for pool or tub use.

Changing rooms are available, and bathing suits are required in the communal pools. There is a nominal charge for renting suits or towels. No credit cards are accepted.

A treaty between the Shoshone and Arapaho nations and the United States specified that the waters were to be free to all. The State Bath House honors this com-

702C STAR PLUNGE
PO Box 627   (307) 864-3771
■ **Thermopolis, WY 82443**

The outdoor swimming pool is maintained at 92-96° and the indoor swimming pool is maintained at 96-98°. The hot pool also has a hydrojet section that is maintained at 104°. Included are an indoor and an outdoor waterslide open throughout the year. The coed steambath is maintained at 118°. All pools are flow-through, requiring only minimal chemical treatment. Bathing suits are required.

Locker rooms and a snack bar are available on the premises. No credit cards are accepted.

Star Plunge provides both indoor and outdoor soaks for all ages.

702D PLAZA HOTEL AND APARTMENTS
PO Box 671   (307) 864-2251
■ **Thermopolis, WY 82443**

An older resort building with men's and women's bathhouses. Each bathhouse has four individual mineral water tubs and two steambaths. Bathing suits are not required in bathhouses.

Hotel rooms, massage, and sweat wraps are available on the premises. Visa and MasterCard are accepted.

702E HOLIDAY INN
PO Box 1323   (307) 864-3131
■ **Thermopolis, WY 82443**

Conventional, major hotel with a unique adaptation of men's and women's bathhouses. Each bathhouse has private spaces for four individual soaking tubs, two saunas and two steambaths. The private spaces are rented to couples, even though they are in the men's and women's bathhouses.

The indoor soaking tubs can be temperature controlled up to 110°, use natural mineral water, and are drained after each use so that no chemical treatment is needed. The outdoor hydrojet pool also uses natural mineral water and is maintained at a temperature of 104°. The outdoor swimming pool uses gas-heated, chlorine-treated tap water and is maintained at a temperature of 81-84°. There is also a private indoor hydropool. All pools and the athletic club facilities are available to the public as well as to registered guests. Bathing suits are required in all outdoor public areas.

Restaurant and hotel rooms are available on the premises. All season sports and equipment rentals are available at the inn or close by. Visa, MasterCard, American Express, and Carte Blanche are accepted.

Present-day explorers have the advantage of a warm, relaxing soak after a hard day fishing or hunting, as did the early settlers to this area.

Hobo Pool: Thanks to the town council, there's not only a fenced swimming pool which charges a fee, but a large soaking pool that is free to everyone.

703   THE SARATOGA INN
PO Box 869   (307) 326-5261
■   **Saratoga, WY 82331**

Modest golf and tennis resort surrounded by rolling ranch country. Elevation 6,800 feet. Open April 1 through October.

Natural mineral water is pumped out of a spring at 114° and piped to an outdoor swimming pool that is treated with chlorine and maintained at 100°. An outdoor, rock soaking pool is built over another spring and is maintained at 100-105°, with chlorine added as needed. Pool use is reserved for registered guests. Bathing suits are required.

Hotel rooms, RV hookups, restaurant, lounge, golf, and tennis are available on the premises. It is four blocks to a store and service station and one mile to overnight camping. Visa, MasterCard, Diners, and American Express are accepted.

Directions: From WY 130 in the town of Saratoga, go east on Bridge Street and follow signs four blocks to the resort.

704   HOBO POOL

●   **In the town of Saratoga**

An improved but unfenced soaking pool and a fenced municipal swimming pool located on the banks of the North Platte River. Elevation 6,800 feet. Open all year.

Natural mineral water flows out of the source spring at 115°. A large cement soaking pool (free to the public) maintains a temperature of 100-110°. Volunteers have channeled the soaking pool runoff into shallow rock pools along the edge of the river. A daily charge is made for the use of the swimming pool, which is maintained at 90°. Bathing suits are required.

There are showers and public rest rooms on the premises. It is three blocks to all services. No credit cards are accepted.

Directions: On WY 130 in the town of Saratoga, watch for the HOBO POOL sign, then follow the signs four blocks east to the pool.

705   ASTORIA MINERAL HOT SPRINGS
(see map below)
Star Route, Box 18   (307) 733-2659
■   **Jackson, WY 83001**

Large, well-kept RV resort on the south bank of the Snake River. Elevation 5,000 feet. Open mid-May to Labor Day.

Natural mineral water flows out of a spring at 104° and is piped to an outdoor swimming pool where it cools naturally and is maintained at a temperature of 95°. The pool is drained and cleaned twice a week, at which time the bottom and sides are treated with chlorine. The pool is available to the public as well as to registered guests who get a discount for pool use. No flotation devices are allowed in the pool. Bathing suits are required.

Locker rooms, picnic area, volleyball, basketball, tent spaces, RV hookups, grocery store, and river raft trips are available on the premises. Bathing suits and towels are available for rent. It is three miles to a service station, store, and motel in Hoback Junction and four miles to a cafe. Visa and MasterCard are accepted.

Location: On US 26/89, 17 miles south of the town of Jackson.

Located on the Snake River (visible below behind the pool) Astoria is a popular stopping place for visitors to Jackson Hole, Grand Tetons, and Yellowstone.

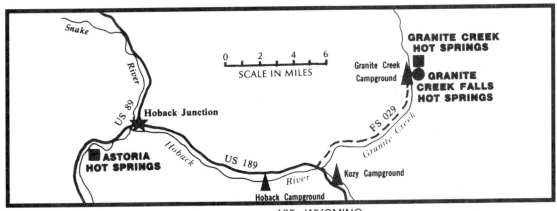

706A GRANITE CREEK HOT SPRINGS
(see map on previous page)

■ **East of Hoback Junction**

Part of a major bonanza for lovers of natural beauty and natural mineral water. Elevation 7,000 feet. Open all year, including the winter season for those who have snow cats.

Natural mineral water flows out of a spring at 112° and tumbles directly into a large cement pool built by the CCC in the 1930s. Cold stream water is added as needed to maintain the pool temperature of 95° in the summer and 105° in the winter. The pool is drained and refilled each day, so no chemical treatment is needed. Bathing suits are required.

Changing rooms and rest rooms are available on the premises, which is operated under a lease with the Forest Service. The site is closed and gates are locked from 8 PM to 10 AM A day-use fee is charged. There is a picnic area with firepits near the pool and a large, wooded, creekside campground .5 miles away. Primitive camping is also available on open stretches at creekside along the 10-mile gravel road between the highway and the springs. It is 18 miles to a cafe and motel and 22 miles to all other services.

Directions: From Jackson, drive south on Hwy 189. Continue bearing left on 189 at Hoback Junction. Follow the road and signs to the pool.

Granite Creek Hot Springs was built by the Civilian Conservation Corps (CCC) in 1933 and is currently operated under a special-use permit granted by the Bridger-Teton National Forest. Located in some of the most beautiful local country and near to many of the area's most popular sights, camping nearby and soaking every evening, the springs offer a treat after hiking and sightseeing. In winter, the pool remains open for those hardy enough to snow-cat in. The soak is worth it!

706B GRANITE CREEK FALLS HOT SPRINGS (see map)

● **East of Hoback Junction**

A series of primitive rock-and-sand soaking pools are located along the creek at the foot of Granite Creek Falls. A small waterfall at 118° seeps up from underground and flows down a creek bank adjacent to Granite Falls and into a series of volunteer-built pools where temperatures range from 96-110°. Temperature can be controlled by diverting the water or by mixing it with cold creek water. These pools must be rebuilt after each annual high-water washout. Although the spring is partly visible from the road, the apparent local custom is clothing optional, although in popular summer months bathing suits seem to be preferred.

Several trails lead to these primitive pools. From the fee-area concrete pool, a trail leads off to the left just before the bridge over the creek. It is a 10 to 15 minute walk along this narrow trail to a spot above the falls where a steep trail heads off to the right down to the creek. Two shallow one-person rock pools are at the foot of the trail. The other pools are to the right toward the falls. These pools can also be reached from the parking area for Granite Falls, which is approximately 10 miles in from the main highway and one mile before the fee-area pool. To reach the pools, it is necessary to ford the very swiftly flowing creek. Do not attempt to ford the creek during high water. A third trail leads up from the Girl Scout Camp parking and trailhead area, which is 7.5 miles in from the highway along the gravel road, before the falls.

While the adults are busy examining some of the warm seeps, this little girl is enjoying one of the several pools located along the swiftly flowing creek, which is dangerous to cross during high water. Other pools are located near the base of Granite Falls.

Kelly Warm Springs: Eighty-one degrees makes this a perfect place for a summer soak—with a perfectly spectacular view of the Grand Tetons.

707   KELLY WARM SPRINGS

● **Northeast of Jackson**

Large warm pond with a gorgeous view of the Grand Tetons, located within the national park. Wonderful for a summer soak. Elevation 6,700 feet. Open all year except for the worst part of winter.

Natural mineral water flows directly into a large gravel-bottom pool up to eight feet deep in an open meadow. The water temperature of 81° makes this an ideal hot-weather soak, albeit a bit cool in winter. The pool is adjacent to the road, so bathing suits are advisable.

There are no services available on the premises. The nearest campground, Gros Ventre, is five miles away in Grand Teton National Park. All other services are 20 miles away in Jackson.

Directions: From Jackson, go north on 26-89-191 about 10 miles to the Gros Ventre junction. Turn right on the unnumbered road to Kelly. From Kelly, drive north one mile and then right again on the road to Slide Lakes. The pond and parking area are less than .5 miles from the junction and are clearly visible from the road.

Source maps: USGS *Shadow Mountain*. (Hot springs not found on Grand Teton National Park map.)

HUCKLEBERRY HOT SPRINGS

The springs were originally developed as a commercial swimming area in the 1960s and continued to operate, free of charge, until the pool was closed by the Park Service in 1983 to let the area return to its natural state. This action included bulldozing the swimming pool and removing the access bridge over Polecat Creek. Now it is necessary to wade Polecat Creek in order to get to the springs from the parking area at the end of the old access road. Trails in the area are not maintained.

In the early morning hours it is easy to find the many springs that dot Huckleberry and Polecat Creeks. All you need to do is look for the rising steam.

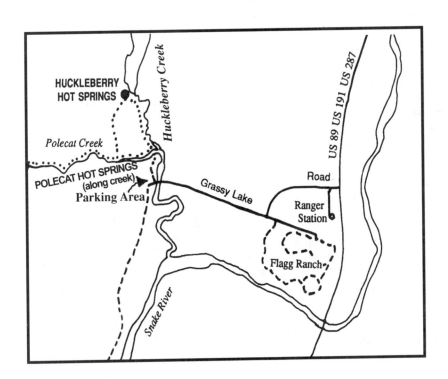

708A HUCKLEBERRY HOT SPRINGS
(see map on previous page)
● **North of the town of Jackson**

Large group of primitive hot springs along the north bank of Polecat Creek within Grand Teton National Park, near the south entrance to Yellowstone National Park. Elevation 6,800 feet. Open all year.

Natural mineral water flows out of many springs at temperatures up to 130°, cooling as it follows various channels to the creek. The hottest and most spectacular flow is where hot water bubbles up into a large pond, flows over hot lava rocks, and tumbles down in a hot waterfall into a soaking pool at 110°. Runoff goes into Huckleberry Creek. The entire creek below this point has hot water, and volunteers have built small rock-and-mud soaking pools at several places where the water is in the 100-105° range. Although this is close to Yellowstone, there are very few visitors, so the apparent local custom is clothing optional. However, it is advisable to have a bathing suit handy in case anyone objects to skinny-dippers.

There are no services available on the premises. There is a commercial campground within one mile, and all other services are available at Flagg Ranch, 1.25 miles away. Flagg Ranch, a private operation, does allow the Park Service to have a Visitors Information office on the premises where some information is provided on the springs and camping areas. Primitive camping areas are also available along Grassy Lake Road, past the turnoff for the springs.

Source map: USGS *Flagg Ranch*; Bridger-Teton National Forest Map (shows springs, but not trails). (Hot springs not shown on Grand Teton National Park map.)

Directions: One-half mile north of Flagg Ranch Village, turn left on Grassy Lake Road for one mile. Immediately after crossing a bridge look for a parking pullout on the right. The trail begins here as an abandoned road. It is a short five-minute walk to Polecat Creek. Wade the creek and continue straight ahead for another 5 to 10 minutes. At a flat grassy area, one trail veers off to the right, leading to the hot creek. Another leads straight ahead to a flat area where water seeps out of the ground just above the scalding waterfall.

Huckleberry Hot Springs: Even though only a few miles from Yellowstone, these pools are rarely crowded. It is possible to enjoy a soak in one of the shallow pools formed by the runoff from the springs towards Polecat Creek or enjoy a natural hot showerbath that empties into a shallow soaking pool.

708B-C POLECAT HOT SPRINGS
(see Huckleberry map)
● **North of the town of Jackson**

Two groups of primitive log-and-rock soaking pools along Polecat Creek, near Huckleberry Creek and hot springs, with spectacular mountain views.

Directions: Driving and access are the same as for Huckleberry Hot Springs. From the parking area, follow the trail to Polecat Creek. After wading the creek, make an immediate left onto a trail which parallels Polecat Creek. It is a short five minute walk to the first group of pools at Lower Polecat.

B: Lower Polecat. A lovely, elaborately elevated log-and-rock soaking pool which is deep enough to sit in and large enough for eight-to-ten people stretched out. Water tumbles through the logs into the pool along the creek where, after mixing with the cool creek water, the soaking temperature is approximately 100°.

C: Upper Polecat. Continue up the trail along the creek for another 15-20 minutes until the trail disappears in a large stand of pine tress. From here, Polecat Creek makes a sweeping curve to the left. Up ahead you will notice a few single pine trees at the creek's edge. Keep your eye on these. The hot pools are at the creek in this area. Walk through the stand of pines, over marshy grassland where the trail virtually disappears, and work your way toward the pine trees along the creek to the pools. (The area is very marshy and difficult to get to in the wet weather.) Hot water seeps out in two separate streams and flows into volunteer-built rock-and-log pools of varying sizes and temperatures as the hot water mixes with cool creek water. (One soaker suggested a stiff brush to clean some of the algae off the rocks.)

Upper Polecat: The marshy grasslands make this a difficult walk, and sometimes algae needs to be cleaned off the logs (see above). But all in all it's a great soak.

Lower Polecat: While soaking alone is sometimes very relaxing, this pool is really large enough to allow eight to ten people to stretch out.

SHOSHONE GEYSER BASIN
In Yellowstone National Park

Several primitive, creekside soaking pools along a beautiful nine-mile trail from Kepler Cascades to the west end of Shoshone Lake.

Boiling hot natural mineral water erupts from geyser cones and bubbles out of hot springs, flowing to join nearby cold streams, the only legal places to put your body in Yellowstone's hot water. Rocks and sand have been arranged by volunteers to make small shallow pools where the two waters combine at temperatures tolerable to human skin. Be sure to check with the rangers to make sure which springs are legal to use.

The view of *Dunanda Falls* from one of the several rock-and-sand pools at the base of the falls is spectacular.

709A   DUNANDA FALLS HOT SPRINGS

● **In Yellowstone National Park**

Several small pools located below the 110-foot Dunanda Falls in a beautifully forested gorge within the Shoshone Geyser Basin area. Elevation 6,500 feet. Access depends on snowpack and spring runoff; could be late June to November.

Natural mineral water flows out of springs adjacent to the river below the falls. The 150° water flows through channels into several rock-and-sand pools at the river's edge, where the temperature can be controlled by mixing with the cold river water. The size and shape of the pools change frequently depending on the degree of flow. The apparent local custom is clothing optional.

There are no services at this location. However, there are several campgrounds in the Shoshone Lake and Shoshone Creek area for which camping permits are required. The springs are adjacent to a primitive campground. Cave Falls Campground is eight miles away. All other services are located 25 miles from the trailhead in Ashton, Idaho.

If you do not already have hiking guides and/or detailed maps of the area, obtain them when you apply for a camping permit. At that time, also ask about weather conditions and any other pertinent information.

Directions: From Ashton, Idaho (ID 20), drive east on Highway 47 and follow the signs 25 miles to the Bechler Ranger Station. This is the trail head for the relatively flat, seven-mile hike to Dunanda Falls.

Ferris Fork: The Bechler River flow reaches approximately one hundred degrees below this major spring.

709B   FERRIS FORK POOL

● **In Yellowstone National Park**

Considered by many to be the "ultimate in hot springs," these multiple rock pools are located halfway between Old Faithful and the Bechler River, .5 miles south of the main trail on a marked spur trail.

Natural mineral water at temperatures up to 190° discharges into the cold water of Shoshone Creek. A pleasant soak for two to three people is possible behind the rocks and logs. Two other similar locations exist nearby. One is a pool on a small side stream just below (south) of the main pool; the other is on Shoshone Creek, just upstream from the main pool. The apparent local custom is clothing optional.

Maps and directions are available from the Ranger Station, and a wilderness permit is required for this easy 16-mile round-trip hike. There are nearby wilderness campgrounds for which a permit is also required.

Ferris Fork Pool is located just south of the major hot-water outflow pictured above.

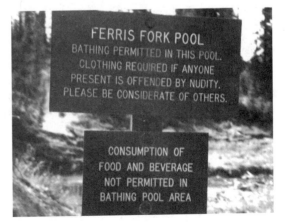

710 MADISON CAMPGROUND WARM SPRING

● **In Yellowstone National Park**

Shallow, mud-bottom ditch near a campground inside the western boundary of Yellowstone National Park. Elevation 6,800 feet. Open all year.

Natural mineral water combined with underground river water bubbles up through a mud flat on the north bank of the Madison River, just south of the campground. Volunteers have built a small sod dam across a narrow channel to accumulate enough 100° water to reach a depth of 18 inches. (The chief ranger wants it known that those volunteers were breaking officially posted park regulation. A sign near these soaking pools reads, "No alteration or digging can be done to the natural flow of the river." The ranger states that anyone caught in the act will be cited and prosecuted.) Bathing suits are required.

Neither ranger at the entrance station to Madison Campgrounds or at the Ranger Information Center near Old Faithful mentioned Madison when asked about where to soak in Yellowstone. However, a sign near the river indicates that soaking is not prohibited though it does issue the following restrictions: Quiet hours are from 8 PM to 8 AM; no soap or shampoo can be used in the area; no alteration or digging...; no food, beverage, or pets are allowed in the area—this is bear country.

No services, other than the campground, are available at the springs. Refer to the NPS Yellowstone Park map for the location of all services in the park.

Directions: Park in the parking area across from campground loop D-E-F and walk 100 yards toward the Madison River and soaking pools. Or park in Loop H and follow the trail (a five-minute walk) to the river and pools.

Boiling River: Probably the best known of the thermal areas in Yellowstone where it is legal to get into the hot water. The strong flow of the current and the scalding hot water flowing in over the banks makes finding a comfortable place to soak a challenge.

711   BOILING RIVER

● **In Yellowstone National Park**

Turbulent confluence of hot mineral water and cold river water along the west bank of the Gardiner River, just below Park Headquarters at Mammoth Hot Spring. Elevation 5,500 feet. Open all year during daylight hours only.

Natural mineral water flows out of a very large spring at 140° and travels 30 yards through an open channel where it tumbles down the south bank of the Gardiner River. Volunteers have rearranged rocks in the river to control the flow of cold water in an eddy pocket where the hot and cold water churn into a swirling mixture that varies from 50-110°. Bathing suits are required.

Facilities include an enclosed pit toilet at the parking area, bear-proof trash receptacles, and a bicycle rack. All other services are available in Gardner, 2.5 miles north; or refer to the NPS Yellowstone Park map for the location of all services within the park.

Directions: On the North Entrance Road between Mammoth Hot Spring and the town of Gardiner, look for a large parking area on both sides of the road at the Montana-Wyoming state line and the 45th Parallel sign. Turn into the parking lot behind that sign on the east side of the road, and hike .5miles upstream to where Boiling River cascades over the riverbank.

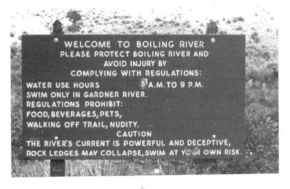

712   MAMMOTH HOT SPRINGS HOTEL AND CABINS
Mammoth Hot Springs (307) 344-7311
Yellowstone National Park, WY 82190

Four fiberglass, hydrojet pools filled with chlorinated, electrically heated tap water behind high board fences adjoining four small cabins. Elevation 6,200 feet. Open all year.

These pools are rented for public use by the hour during the winter. During the summer they are for the private use of the registered guests in each of the four cabins. Phone for rates and reservations.

STATES EAST OF THE ROCKIES

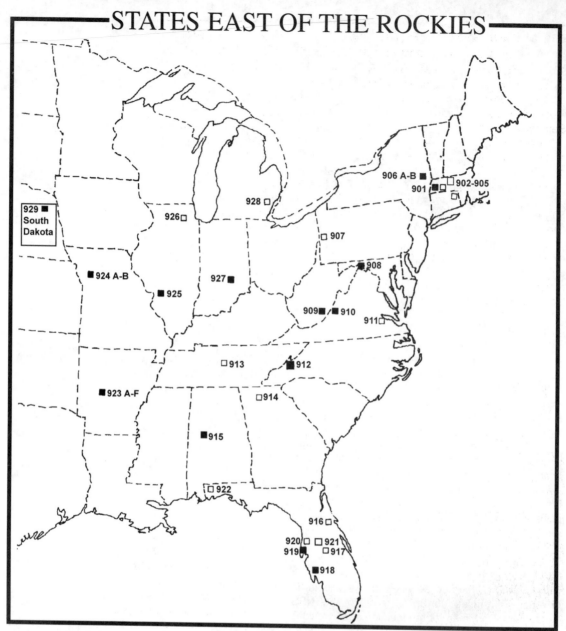

This map was designed to be used with a standard highway map.

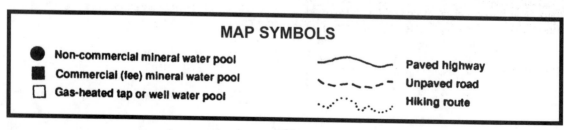

MAP SYMBOLS

● Non-commercial mineral water pool
■ Commercial (fee) mineral water pool
□ Gas-heated tap or well water pool

～ Paved highway
- - - Unpaved road
⋯⋯ Hiking route

901 SAND SPRINGS POOL
Sand Springs Road   (413) 458-5205
■ **Williamstown, MA 01267**

An historic seasonal plunge located in the heart of the Berkshire Hills in northwestern Massachusetts. Elevation 900 feet. Open May-September.

Natural mineral water flows out of a spring at 74° and is piped to several pools where it is gas-heated and treated with chlorine. The whirlpool is maintained at a temperature of 102°. The swimming pool and toddler's pool are maintained at approximately 80°. A grass beach for lounging is a pleasant addition. Bathing suits are required.

Facilities include changing rooms, sundeck, exercise room, sauna, snack bar, dance floor, picnic tables, and large lawn. A motel, service station, restaurant and other services are available within 10 blocks. No credit cards are accepted.

Directions: From the Williamstown municipal building on US 7, drive north to Sand Springs Rd. Turn right and follow signs to pool.

Sand Springs Pool: This would be the perfect place for a retreat from the heat during a New England summer.

902 THE SPA
414 Mohawk Trail   (413) 774-2951
☐ **Greenfield, MA 01301 800-THESPA-1**

Beautiful, modern spa with outdoor redwood deck offering a three-state view, located at the gateway to the Berkshires.

Sunken tubs in two indoor private rooms offer individual showers, adjustable air and water jets, and variable lighting, and can accommodate up to six people. The one outdoor tub offers a breathtaking vies. The tubs are maintained at 102° and chlorine treated. Handicap access is available with help.

Massage, a Turkish steambath, tanning rooms, and a sauna are available on the premises along with a juice bar, lounging nooks and games. Special "pampering" packages are available as are private party rentals. Major credit cards are accepted. Phone for rates, reservations and directions.

903 EAST HEAVEN TUB CO.
33 West St.   (413) 586-6843
☐ **Northampton, MA 01060**

Beautiful, Japanese-motif rental facility located across from Smith College in the Connecticut Valley.

Private-space hot pools using gas-heated tap water treated with bromine are for rent to the public. There are four indoor tubs in private rooms and three outdoor tubs in private, roofless enclosures on the roof. All are maintained at a temperature of 104°.

Sales of saunas, hot tubs and spas are conducted on the premises. No credit cards are accepted. Phone for rates, reservations and directions.

904 SPA OF AMHERST
175ND University Drive (413)253-7727
☐ **Amherst, MA 01002**

New rental facility located near the University of Massachusetts in central Amherst.

Private-space hot pools using gas-heated tap water treated with bromine are for rent to the public. There are four indoor private-space tubs which are maintained at a temperature of 102-104°.

Facilities include four tanning beds. Massage is available on the premises. Visa, MasterCard, American Express and Discover are accepted.

Phone for rates, reservations and directions.

905 SOLAIR RECREATION LEAGUE
PO Box 187   (203) 928-9174
☐   Southbridge, MA 01550

A family nudist campground with its own private lake, located on 350 hilly acres in northeast Connecticut. Elevation 600 feet. Open to visitors from April to November.

The hydrojet tub in the clubhouse uses gas-heated well water treated with bromine and is maintained at 104°. Clothing is prohibited in the pool and beach area, optional elsewhere.

Facilities include hiking trails, a private lake for swimming and boating, a clubhouse with an electric sauna, a wood-fired sauna, a shower building, a large game room, dining hall, tennis and volleyball courts, horseshoe pits, and children's playground. Rental cabins, RV hookups, and tent spaces are on the premises. No credit cards are accepted. It is four miles to a store and service station.

Note: This is a membership organization not open to the public for drop-in visits, but interested visitors may be issued a guest pass by prior arrangement. Telephone or write for information and directions.

THE SPRINGS OF SARATOGA

The Saratoga Springs area has a two-century-old tradition of providing natural beauty, health giving geothermal water, and the gaiety of its summer racetrack season. More than a dozen springs and hot wells discharge naturally carbonated mineral water along the Saratoga Fault, which is located in a low basin between Lake George and Albany.

In 1909 the state of New York created a Reservation Commission and acquired the land around Geyser Creek, which has now been designated as Saratoga Spa State Park. Some geothermal activities are still accessible for public viewing, such as the only spouting geyser east of the Mississippi River.

Bathing in mineral water is available only at the Lincoln and Roosevelt bathhouses in the Park and at the Crystal Spa bathhouse in the city of Saratoga Springs. All bathhouses have separate men's and women's sections using one-person tubs that are drained and filled after each use so that no chemical treatment of the water is necessary.

906A ROOSEVELT BATHHOUSE
(518) 584-2011
■   Saratoga Springs, NY 12866

Large, traditional state-owned bathhouse with nearby hotel and conference center operated by TW Services. Open all year.

Mineral water flows out of a spring at 52° and is piped to individual tubs in private rooms. Along the way it is heated to 99°, the maximum permitted in the state-owned bathhouse.

Hot packs and massage are also available on the premises.

Credit cards are not accepted. Phone for rates, reservations and directions.

The Crystal Spa: This genuine Victorian gazebo and costuming is reminiscent of ladies and gents coming to "take the waters" during the racing season.

906B CRYSTAL SPA
92 S. Broadway   (518) 584-2556
■   Saratoga Springs, NY 12866

Newly constructed, privately owned spa associated with the Grand Union Motel where the mineral water is available for drinking as well as for bathing. Open all year.

Mineral water flows out of a spring at 52° and is piped to individual soaking tubs where it is mixed with 149° tap water as needed to obtain the desired soaking temperature. Separate facilities are provided for men and women.

New building additions offer expanded services. Sauna, massage, facials, manicures, and pedicures are available on the premises. Pampering packages are available. No credit cards are accepted. Phone for rates, reservations, and directions.

907 WHITE THORN LODGE
RD #1, Box 242   (412) 846-5984
☐   **Darlington, PA 96115**

A 106-acre, member-owned nudist park located in western Pennsylvania near the Ohio state line, 50 miles from downtown Pittsburg. Elevation 1,000 feet. Open for visitors May through September.

The outdoor hot tub using electrically heated well water treated with bromine is maintained at 105°. The swimming pool, using sun-heated well water treated with bromine, varies in temperature. Nudity is expected, weather permitting, everywhere on the grounds.

Facilities include hiking trails, rooms, RV hookups, camping spaces, clubhouse, sauna, weekend snack bar, tennis and volleyball courts, horseshoe pits, junior clubhouse, and play area. No credit cards are accepted.

Note: This is a membership organization not open to the public for visits, but interested visitors may be issued a guest pass by prior arrangement. Telephone or write for information and directions.

908 BERKELEY SPRINGS STATE PARK
(304) 258-2711
■   **Berkeley Springs, WV 25411**

Large, traditional bathhouse and plunge operated as a state park, located in a narrow valley in West Virginia's eastern panhandle. Elevation 620 feet. Open 362 days per year.

Two thousand gallons-per-minute of mineral water flow out of several springs at a temperature of 74°. A portion of this water is steam-heated to 102° and piped to private, one-person bathtubs in the main bathhouse and to private tiled baths in the Old Roman Bath House. All are drained and refilled after each use so that no chemical treatment of the water is necessary. The Old Roman Bath House is open weekends all year and daily from Memorial Day to Columbus Day. Mineral spring water is also piped directly to the outdoor swimming pool, which is treated with chlorine and is open from Memorial Day through Labor Day.

Facilities include steam cabinets. Massage, heat treatments, and other health services are available on the premises. Visa and Mastercard are accepted. All other services are available in the adjoining town of Berkeley Springs. Phone for rates, reservations, and directions.

Berkeley Springs State Park: I wonder what the ancient Romans would have to say about the coed soaks at the Old Roman Bath House?

The Greenbrier, offers the ultimate in luxurious accommodations and facilities.

909   THE GREENBRIER

(800) 624-6070
(304) 536-1110

■   **White Sulphur Springs, WV 24986**

A large, historic, health-oriented mineral spring resort occupying 6,500 acres in an upland valley of the Allegheny Mountains, near the Virginia border. Elevation 2,900 feet. Open all year.

Natural mineral water flows out of a sulphur spring at 58° and is piped to individual soaking tubs in separate men's and women's sections of the mineral-bath wing, where it is heated by electricity to the desired temperature. Tubs are drained and filled after each use, so no chemical treatment is needed. Water from a fresh-water spring is piped to an outdoor pool and the Grand Indoor Pool, where it is treated with chlorine and heated by steam to a temperature of 75°. Bathing suits are required.

Facilities include rooms and luxury suites, dining rooms and restaurants, a complete convention center, shops, service station, tennis courts, three golf courses, aerobics studio, exercise equipment, beauty salon, and a complete diagnostic clinic. Services include fitness evaluations, massage, herbal wrap, facials, manicures, and pedicures. The diagnostic clinic and shops are available to the public. All other facilities are for the use of registered guests only. Visa, MasterCard, American Express and Diners Club are accepted. Phone or write for rates, reservations, and directions.

The Homestead: The flow of water at the source spring is so great that several pools can be maintained on a flow-through basis at this 15,000 acre up-scale resort.

910   THE HOMESTEAD
(703) 839-5500

■   **Hot Springs, VA 24445**

A very large, very historic, luxurious resort on the west slope of the Allegheny Mountains near the West Virginia Border. Elevation 2,500 feet. Open all year.

The odorless mineral water used at the Homestead Spa flows from several springs at temperatures ranging from 102-106°. It is piped to individual, one-person bathtubs in separate men's and women's bathhouses, where it is mixed to provide an ideal temperature of 104°. Tubs are drained and refilled after each use so that no chemical treatment of the water is necessary. Mineral water from the same springs is used in an indoor swimming pool maintained at 84° and an outdoor swimming pool maintained at 72°. Both pools receive a minimum of chlorine treatment. Use of the spa and all pools is restricted to registered guests only. Bathing suits are required except as indicated in the bathhouses.

Five miles away but still within the 15,000-acre Homestead property are the Warm Springs, which flow at 96°. The rate of discharge is so great that the two large Warms Springs pools, in separate men's and women's buildings, maintain a temperature of 96° on a flow-through basis, requiring no chemical treatment of the water. These Warm Springs pools are open only during the warm months and are open to the public. Bathing suits are optional.

The facilities include 600 bedrooms and parlors, restaurants, shops, conference center, bowling alley, movie theater, and tennis courts. Recreational activities available on the premises include golf, archery, fishing, hiking, riding, skeet and trap shooting, and tennis, plus skiing and ice skating in the winter. There are many resort services available, some of which are included in the basic room rate. Phone or write for complete information. Visa, MasterCard, and American Express are accepted.

911 WHITE TAIL PARK

PO Box 160   (804) 859-6123
☐   Zuni, VA 23898

Large (47-acre), well-equipped family nudist park located in southeastern Virginia, 35 miles from I-95 and 45 miles from Norfolk. Elevation 39 feet. Open all year.

A large, indoor spa/hot tub is filled with gas-heated well water treated with bromine and maintained at 104°. The outdoor swimming pool is filled with solar-heated well water treated with Baquacil and maintained in the low 80s from April to November. This is a nudist resort, so everyone is expected to be nude, weather and health permitting.

Facilities include 17 mobile home living sites, nature trail, recreation hall, children's rec center, game courts, rooms, tent spaces, RV hookups, and seasonal snack bar. Visa and MasterCard are accepted. It is four miles to all other services.

Note: This is a membership organization, but the park will accept drop-in visitors anytime. Telephone or write for information and directions.

912 HOT SPRINGS SPA

PO Box 428   (704) 622-7676
■   Hot Springs, NC 28743

Picturesque rustic spa and campground on the banks of the French Broad River in the mountains near the Tennessee border. Elevation 2,000 feet. Open all year.

Natural mineral water flows out of a spring at 100° and is piped to six outdoor soaking pools scattered through a wooded area along the river. Pools are drained and refilled after each use, so no chemical treatment of the water is required. One of the pools is equipped with a plastic bubble for winter use. Bathing suits are officially required, but some of the pools are very secluded.

Facilities include RV hookups and a service station. Massage is available on the premises. All other services are available .25 miles away in the town. Visa and MasterCard are accepted.

Phone for rates, reservations, and directions.

913 ROCK HAVEN LODGE

PO Box 1291   (615) 896-3553
☐   Murfreesboro, TN 37133

A traditional, family nudist park with a country atmosphere, located on 25 wooded acres 40 miles from Nashville. Elevation 650 feet. Open for visitors April 1 to October 31.

One large, outdoor whirlpool spa using chlorine-treated well water is maintained at 103°, and one outdoor unheated swimming pool using similar water averages over 70° in the summer. Clothing is prohibited in pools. This is a nudist park, not a clothing-optional resort, so members and guests are expected to be nude, weather permitting.

Facilities include rental cabins, a country store, RV hookups, camping area, clubhouse, and volleyball, tennis and other sports courts. It is six miles to restaurants and motels.

Note: This is a membership organization, but the park will accept drop-in first-time visitors anytime. Telephone or write for information and directions.

914 HIDDEN VALLEY RESORT, INC.

Rt. 3, Box 3452   (706) 265-6110
☐   Dawsonville, GA 30534

A secluded, heavily wooded nudist resort nestled in the scenic foothills of the North Georgia Mountains. Elevation 1,500 feet. Open mid-March through early December.

Gas-heated well water treated with bromine and chlorine, is used in an enclosed outdoor hydropool that comfortably holds 24 and is maintained at 104°. A spacious cement-and-rock-lined pond, fed by a running mountain stream, maintains a temperature of 65°. A large, free-form swimming pool fed by a waterfall and surrounded with concrete decking is also available. Clothing is prohibited in all pools. This is a nudist club, not a clothing-optional resort, so nudity is generally expected everywhere, weather permitting.

Facilities include rental rooms and housekeeping units, RV spaces, camping area, seasonal snack bar, volleyball, tennis, and shuffleboard courts. Visa and MasterCard are accepted. It is five miles to a store and restaurant.

This is a family-oriented club that accepts singles on a reservation basis only. Membership is not required to visit, and couples and families may visit without making reservations. Phone or write for further information and directions.

915 COTTONWOOD HOT SPRINGS SPA AND MOTEL
600 Hot Springs Rd. (205) 691-4101
■ **Cottonwood, AL (800) 526-SPAS**

A full range of health services is offered by this destination motel and spa located on nine hundred acres with full recreational facilities.

Two outdoor, hot, mineral water swimming pools and eight indoor, private, mineral tubs are fed by hot salt mineral water piped above ground from a drilling depth of almost one mile. The temperature in the swimming pool is 112°, and the temperature in the private pools is kept at 90°.

Motel rooms and suites, RV hook-ups, a restaurant, conference center, lake, fishing, bicycle and nature walks, picnic area, a golf driving range, massage, and health food store and gift shop are all available on the premises. It is also possible to book family reunions and retreats. Major credit cards are accepted. Phone for rates, reservations, and directions.

Cottonwood Hot Springs: The hot mineral water to fill this pool comes from 4,800 feet under the earth.

Cypress Cove provides a beautiful scenic place to paint nature "au naturel."

916 SUNNY SANDS RESORT
502 Central Blvd. (904) 749-2233
□ **Pierson, FL 32080**

Fifty acres of rustic woods surrounding a private lake, located 20 miles north of Deland in northeastern Florida. Elevation 20 feet. Open all year.

The outdoor hydrojet spa is filled with gas-heated well water treated with bromine and maintained at 103°. The swimming pool is filled with heated well water, treated with chlorine, and the temperature varies with the seasons. Clothing is prohibited in the pools, and nudity is expected elsewhere, weather and health permitting.

Facilities include mobilehome rentals, RV hook-ups, tent spaces, recreation hall, fishing, volleyball and shuffleboard courts, horseshoe pit, and playground. Visa and MasterCard are accepted. It is 20 miles to Deland and all other services.

Note: This is a membership organization open for drop-in visits by couples or families. Telephone or write for more information and directions.

917 CYPRESS COVE NUDIST RESORT
4425 Pleasant Hill Rd (407) 933-5870
□ **Kissimmee, FL 34746**

Beautiful, large, modern, clothes-free destination resort surrounding a private 50-acre lake in central Florida, within 30 minutes of Disney World, Cypress Gardens, and Sea World. Because this is a family resort, most visitors are married couples, many with children. Singles are also welcomed when accompanied by a member of the opposite sex. Elevation 77 feet. Open all year.

Well water heated by gas is piped to the outdoor pool. The whirlpool spa is heated to 103° and treated with bromine. The swimming pool is heated to 80° and treated with chlorine. Nudity is expected in the pool areas, everyone dresses for the Saturday night dances, and clothing is optional at other times and places, according to comfort and to suit the occasion.

Motel rooms, apartments, RV spaces, restaurant, poolside bar, and paddleboats for the lake are available on the premises. Activities such as exercise and yoga classes, tennis clinics, and craft classes are also available. It is one mile to a service station and market. Visa and MasterCard are accepted.

Directions: South of Orlando, follow US 17-92 three miles south of Kissimmee to FL 531 (Pleasant Hill Road). Turn left eight miles to Cypress Cove.

Safety Harbor: Workshops and meals to improve your health and beautify you inside and out are offered in these luxurious surroundings. There are also programs to entertain your children while you are stretching and soaking.

918 RESORT AND SPA AT WARM MINERAL SPRINGS
San Servando Ave. (813) 426-9581
■ **Warm Mineral Springs, FL 34287**

Modern spa, health studio, and nearby apartment complex with a nine-million-gallons-per-day mineral spring, located halfway between Fort Meyers and Sarasota. Elevation 10 feet. Open all year.

Mineral water flows out of the ground at 87° and into a two-acre private lake. It is also piped to a health studio. The lake, which is used for swimming, does not need chlorination because of the volume of flow-through mineral water. The indoor soaking tubs and whirlpool baths are filled with 87° water. The tubs are drained and refilled after each use so that no chemical treatment is needed. Bathing suits are required except in private rooms.

Facilities include sauna, gift shop, post office, bakery and snack bar. Massage, hot pack, medical examinations, and nearby apartment rentals are available on the premises. No credit cards are accepted. Phone for rates, reservations, and directions.

919 SAFETY HARBOR SPA AND FITNESS CENTER
105 N. Bayshore Dr. 800-237-0155
■ **Safety Harbor, FL 34695**

An upscale, historic spa recently refurbished, specializing in fitness and beauty programs, located at the west end of Tampa Bay. Elevation 10 feet. Open all year.

Natural mineral water flows from four springs at approximately 55° and is piped to several pools and to separate men's and women's bathhouses. Gas is used to heat the water as needed. The six individual soaking tubs in the men's and women's bathhouses are drained and filled after each use so that no chemical treatment of the water is necessary. All other pools are treated with chlorine. The courtyard swimming pool, the lap pool, the indoor exercise pool and the women's pool are maintained at 85°. Two coed hydrojet pools are maintained at 99° and 101°. Bathing suits are not required in bathhouses.

Facilities include fitness center, tennis courts, golf driving range, guest rooms, dining room and conference center. Tennis and golf lessons, exercise classes, medical and nutritional consultation, massage, herbal wraps, skin care treatment and complete beauty salon services are available on the premises. All facilities and services are reserved for the use of registered guests only. Visa, MasterCard, American Express, and Diner Club, are accepted.

Phone for rates, reservations, and directions.

City Retreat: Even the name of this nudist park invites you to get away and enjoy the pools and fun on the peaceful tree-shaded 40 acres.

920 CITY RETREAT NUDIST PARK
13220 Houston Ave.   (813) 868-1061
☐   Hudson, FL 34667

Forty acres of tree-shaded nudist tranquility in a grassy-sandy country setting, 45 miles north of Tampa. Elevation 30 feet. Open all year.

The outdoor hydrospa is filled with gas-heated well water treated with chlorine, and maintained at 101-103°. The outdoor pool is filled with heated well water maintained at 82° and is treated with chlorine. Clothing is prohibited in the pool and spa area. This is a nudist club, not a clothing-optional resort. Clothing is not allowed in the pool area. Everyone dresses according to the weather.

Facilities include a club house, motel rooms, campers, mobile homes, tenting spaces, RV hook-ups, snack bar, tennis court, and shuffleboard courts. Visa and MasterCard are accepted. It is five miles to a shopping center.

Note: We are family oriented; however anyone with a sincere interest in nudism is welcome. Phone for information, rates and directions.

921 PARADISE LAKES
PO Box 750   (813) 949-9327
☐   Land O'Lakes, FL 34639

A clothing-optional vacation resort for the whole family with its own lake and beautifully decorated grounds and buildings. Elevation 30 feet. Open all year.

Two outdoor swimming pools, one reserved for volleyball, are heated to 78°, while the indoor pool is kept at 85°. The large 70-foot spa is maintained at 95° and the small spa at 104°. All pools are chlorine treated.

Accommodations include poolside hotel rooms, deluxe suites with private hot tubs, condos, and a full-hookup RV park. Facilities include a first-class restaurant and bar, fitness rooms, massage, sauna, tennis, and canoeing, fishing, or paddle boating on the lake.

Located 17 miles north of Tampa on Highway 41. All major credit cards are accepted. Phone for rates, directions, and reservations.

922 ETHOS TRACE, INC.
PO Box 2233   (904) 994-3665
☐   Pace, FL 32571

A 16-acre tree-shaded, family-oriented nudist park, located near Pensacola and I-10 in the Florida panhandle. Elevation 120 feet. Open all year.

The outdoor hydrojet spa and swimming pool are filled with gas-heated city water treated with chlorine. The spa is maintained at 102°. This is a nudist park, so members and visitors are expected to be nude, weather permitting.

Facilities include RV hookups, camping spaces, lighted volleyball courts, horseshoe pits and sunning lawns. No credit cards are accepted. All other services are available within five miles.

Interested visitors are welcome and singles are admitted. A daily "ground fee" entitles each visitor to use the pools and all other recreational facilities. Phone for rates, reservations, and directions.

Hernando De Soto may or may not have been the first European on the scene, but today's Hot Springs National Park and the surrounding community have their roots in the 1803 Louisiana Purchase. In 1832, Congress took the unprecedented step of establishing public ownership by setting aside four sections of land as a reservation. Unfortunately, no one adequately identified the exact boundaries of this reservation, so the mid-19th century was filled with conflicting claims and counterclaims to the springs and surrounding land.

By 1870, a system evolved that reserved the springs for the Federal Government and sold the developed land to the persons who had settled it. At the same time, the government agreed to collect the 143-degree geothermal spring water into a central distribution system that carried it to private property establishments where baths were offered to the public. By 1877, all primitive soaking "pits" along Hot Springs Creek were eliminated when the creek was confined to a concrete channel, roofed over, and then paved to create what is now Central Avenue.

In 1921, The Federal Reservation became Hot Springs National Park, custodian of all the springs and the exclusive contractual supplier of hot mineral water to those elaborate establishments that had become the famous Bathhouse Row. It is also the authority that approves every establishment's rates, equipment, personnel and services related to that water.

In 1949, the Park Service installed air-cooled radiators and tap-water cooled heat exchangers to supply a new central "cool" mineral water reservoir. Now all thermal water customers receive their supply through two pipes, "hot" at 143° and "'cool" at 90°.

During the last four decades, declining patronage forced the closure of many of those historic temples built for "taking the waters." However, the last several years has seen a large resurgence of interest in thermal soaking both for therapy and for pure relaxation, so many of the historic Bathhouse Row locations are being refurbished.

For additional information contact the Hot Springs Chamber of Commerce, PO Box 1500, Hot Springs, AR 71902.

923A   BUCKSTAFF BATHS

■   **(501) 623-2308**

One of the historic Bathhouse Row establishments in continuous operation since 1912, located at the south end of the Row near the Visitor Center.

Separate men's and women's sections offer one-person soaking tubs that are individually temperature-controlled. They are drained and refilled after each use so no chemical treatment of the water is needed. Whirlpool baths and massage are available.

Facilities include a third-floor coed lounge with separate men's and women's sun decks at each end. No credit cards are accepted.

In response to the increased interest in stress reduction these three soakers are enjoying a relaxing time after work in one of the large soaking pools at *Libbey Memorial*, one of the only concessioners actually located in Hot Springs National Park.

923B LIBBEY MEMORIAL PHYSICAL MEDICINE CENTER AND HOT SPRINGS HEALTH SPA

(501) 321-1997

Downstairs, a modern, "Medicare-approved, federally regulated" therapy facility and, upstairs, a modern spa with coed soaking tubs, located on Reserve Avenue, three blocks east of Central Avenue.

The Libbey Memorial coed thermal whirlpool (105°) and coed exercise pool (98°) are drained and refilled each day, so no chemical treatment of the water is necessary. Facilities include steam and vapor cabinets and electric hoists at therapy pools. Hot packs, massage, and prescribed treatments such as Paraffin Immersion, Ultra Sound Therapy, and Electric Stimulation are also available. No credit cards are accepted.

The health spa's eight large coed soaking tubs are individually temperature-controlled as desired between 102° and 108°. All are drained and filled each day so that no chemical treatment of the water is necessary. Children are welcome. Massage, steam and vapor cabinets, sun beds, and exercise equipment are available. No credit cards are accepted.

Catering to therapy needs downstairs and recreational fun upstairs, *Libbey Memorial* appeals to the total hot mineral water marketplace.

HOT TUB

NATURALLY-HEATED THERMAL WATERS

FROM THE 47 SPRINGS

OF OUR NATIONAL PARK

Water from these springs has been keeping people warm since 1875, when the original Arlington Hotel was opened. The present Arlington Resort opened with a gala New Year's Eve party in 1924. The famous President Teddy Roosevelt and the infamous gangster Al Capone have both stayed here.

923C ARLINGTON RESORT HOTEL & SPA (800) 643-1502
■ In Arkansas (501) 623-7771

A magnificent, luxurious resort in a dominant location overlooking the downtown historic district and Bathhouse Row in Hot Springs National Park.

The in-hotel bathhouse with separate men's and women's sections is open to hotel guests and the public. Private soaking tubs are individually temperature-controlled and drained after each use so that no chemical treatment of the water is necessary. Massage, hot packs, saunas, sitz-baths, steam baths, and needle showers are available.

A mineral-water redwood hot tub, two tap water swimming pools treated with chlorine, and a multi-level sundeck are reserved for registered guests. The hot tub is maintained at 104°, and the twin pools are maintained at 86° year round.

Facilities include three restaurants and two lounges, beauty and facial salon, exercise room, ballroom, conference and exhibit centers, and shopping mall. Visa, MasterCard, American Express, and Discover are accepted.

923D DOWNTOWNER HOTEL & SPA (800) 251-1962
■ (501) 624-5521

A modern hotel with a large second-floor bathhouse, located on Central Avenue, one block north of Bathhouse Row.

A bathhouse with separate men's and women's sections is open to the public. One-person soaking tubs are individually temperature-controlled and drained after each use so that no chemical treatment of the water is necessary. Whirlpool baths, vapor treatments, hot packs, sitz baths, and massage are available.

An outdoor swimming pool and a hot tub are filled with chlorine-treated tap water, and are reserved for the use of registered guests.

Facilities include a beauty salon, sun decks and two restaurants. Visa, MasterCard, American Express and Discover are accepted.

923E   HOT SPRINGS HILTON
(800) HILTONS
In Arkansas (501) 623-6600

■

Large, modern resort hotel located next to the Hot Springs Convention Center, two blocks south of Bathhouse Row.

A bathhouse with separate men's and women's sections is open to the public. One-person soaking tubs are individually temperature-controlled and drained after each use so that no chemical treatment of the water is necessary. Massage is available.

An indoor whirlpool (108°) and an indoor-outdoor swimming pool filled with chlorine-treated tap water are reserved for the use of registered guests.

Facilities include restaurants, lounge, meeting rooms and banquet facilities. Visa, MasterCard, American Express, Diners Club, and Discover are accepted.

923F   MAJESTIC RESORT/SPA
(800) 643-1504
In Arkansas (501) 623-5511

■

A unique combination of hotel, motel, and health spa facilities located at the north end of Central Avenue.

A bathhouse with separate men's and women's sections is open to the public. Individual soaking tubs are temperature-controlled and drained after each use so that no chemical treatment of the water is necessary. Massage is available.

An outdoor swimming pool filled with chlorine-treated tap water and heated in the winter is reserved for the use of registered guests.

Facilities include deluxe rooms and suites, beauty salon, two restaurants and a lounge, old fashioned soda fountain, gift and clothing shops, and conference and banquet rooms. Visa, MasterCard, American Express, and Discover are accepted.

Elms Resort Hotel: This couple is enjoying a soak in one of the beautifully decorated theme rooms; this one even has a waterfall to enhance the ambience.

924A EXCELSIOR SPRINGS MINERAL WATER SPA

Hall of Waters   **(816) 637-0753**
■ **Excelsior Springs, MO 64024**

A large, historic building originally constructed for health-oriented activities is now owned and operated on a limited scale by the city. Elevation 900 feet. Open weekdays only.

Cold (54°) natural mineral water is pumped from wells (which used to be flowing springs) and piped to a bathhouse where it is gas-heated and used in four individual, private-space tubs. After each use, tubs are drained and refilled so that no chemical treatment of the water is necessary. The bathhouse is for men only in the morning and women only in the afternoon. Steambaths and massage are available on the premises. The indoor swimming pool, using gas-heated, chlorine-treated tap water, is maintained at approximately 75° and open only in the summer. Bathing suits are required in this coed pool.

Facilities include dressing rooms and a water bar where mineral water is sold by the gallon. Visa and MasterCard are accepted. Phone for rates, reservations, and directions.

924B THE ELMS RESORT HOTEL

Regent and Elms Blvd. (816) 630-2141
■ **Excelsior Springs, MO 64024**

An historic luxury resort on 23 wooded acres, one-half hour northeast of Kansas City. Elevation 900 feet. Open all year.

Cold (54°) natural mineral water is pumped from wells on the property and piped to single soaking tubs in separate men's and women's sections of the elaborate New Leaf Spa. Customers control tub water temperature by adding hot tap water to the cold mineral water as desired. The tubs are drained and filled after each use so no chemical treatment of the water is necessary.

Chlorine-treated tap water is used in all other pools. There are six theme rooms, each containing environmental effects and a two-person soaking tub in which water temperature is controllable. The indoor European swimming track is maintained at 75°, the three large, outdoor hot tub pools are maintained at 100°, and the outdoor swimming pool is solar heated. Bathing suits are required in these public-area coed pools. The New Leaf Spa is open to the public as well as to registered guests.

New Leaf Spa services include steambaths, jogging track, saunas, beauty shop, exercise room, herbal wrap, and massage. Other facilities include rooms, suites, condos, restaurant, and various sports courts. Visa, MasterCard, American Express, and Diners Club are accepted. Phone for rates, reservations, and directions.

925 THE ORIGINAL SPRINGS HOTEL AND BATH HOUSE
(618) 243-5458
■ **Okawville, IL 62271**

An authentic turn-of-the-century mineral spring resort hotel, located in a small town on I-64, 41 miles east of St. Louis. Elevation 600 feet. Open all year.

Natural mineral water flows out of a spring at approximately 50° and is piped to separate men's and women's bathhouses, where it is gas-heated as needed in one-person soaking tubs. Tubs are drained and filled after each use so no chemical treatment of the water is necessary. The indoor/outdoor swimming pool uses gas-heated tap water treated with chlorine, and is maintained at 85°. Bathing suits are not required in bathhouses. Day use customers are welcome.

Facilities include guest rooms and a restaurant. Massage is available on the premises. Visa, MasterCard, Discover and American Express are accepted. It is less than four blocks to a service station, store and other services.

Phone for rates, reservations, and directions.

926 CLEARWATER HOT TUBS
1201 Butterfield Rd. (708) 852-7676
□ **Downers Grove, IL 60515**

A user-friendly, rent-a-tub facility located in a suburban town 25 miles west of Chicago.

Private-space redwood hot tubs using gas-heated tap water are treated with bromine. Four of the twelve units are VIP suites with TV and oversized tubs suitable for large groups. Four have a sauna and a loft area. Pool temperatures are maintained at approximately 100° in the summer and 104° in the winter. Clothing is optional in the private spaces and required elsewhere.

Massage with steam room is available by appointment. Visa, MasterCard, American Express, and Discover Card are accepted. Phone for rates, reservations, and directions.

927 FRENCH LICK SPRINGS RESORT
(812) 936-9300
■ **French Lick, IN 47432**

The "largest most complete resort in the Midwest," located on 2,600 wooded acres in southwest Indiana, two hours from Indianapolis. Elevation 600 feet. Open all year.

Natural mineral water flows from a spring at 50° and is piped to separate men's and women's bathhouses where it is heated by gas-generated steam, as needed, for one-person soaking tubs. Tubs are drained and filled after each use so no chemical treatment of the water is necessary. All other pools use steam-heated tap water treated with chlorine. The outdoor and indoor whirlpools are maintained at 104°, the dome pool ranges from 72° in the summer to 82° in the winter, and the Olympic swimming pool, for summer use only, is not heated. Bathing suits are required except in bathhouses.

Facilities include two 18-hole golf courses, indoor and outdoor tennis courts, equestrian stables and riding trails, guest rooms, nine restaurants and lounges, bowling alleys, conference center, exercise facility, and beauty salon. Massage, body treatments, saunas, steambaths, reflexology, salt rubs, facials, and manicures are available on the premises. Visa, MasterCard, and American Express are accepted. It is three blocks to a service station, store, and other services.

Phone for rates, reservations, and directions.

928 WHISPERING OAKS
5864 Baldwin (313) 628-2676
□ **Oxford, MI 48371**

A traditional nudist resort on 52 acres of beautiful rolling woodland with a private lake, 35 miles north of Detroit. Elevation 1,200 feet. Open April to October.

The outdoor whirlpool spa is filled with propane-heated well water treated with chlorine and maintained at 105°. The outdoor diving pool is filled with propane-heated well water treated with chlorine and maintained at 80°. This is a nudist facility, so everyone is expected to be nude weather and health permitting.

Facilities include sauna, clubhouse, RV hookups, tent spaces, and volleyball, tennis, and shuffleboard courts. Visa and MasterCard are accepted. It is five miles to a service station, cafe, and motel.

Note: This is a membership organization not open to the public for drop-in visits, but prospective members may be issued a guest pass by prior arrangement. Telephone for further information.

929   EVANS PLUNGE
1145 North River   (605) 745-5165
■   **Hot Springs, SD 57747**

The world's largest natural warm water indoor swimming pool and water park, located at the north edge of the town of Hot Springs in southwestern South Dakota. Elevation 3,800 feet. Open all year.

Five thousand gallons per minute of 87° water rises out of the pebble bottom of the plunge, providing a complete change of water 16 times daily, so only a minimum of chlorine is necessary. Waterslides, traveling rings, fun tubes, and kiddie pools are available at the plunge. Two hydrojet spas (100-104°), sauna, steam room, and fitness equipment are located in the health club. No credit cards are accepted.

A gift shop is available on the premises. All other services are available within .5 miles.

Evans Plunge: Less than 60 miles from Mt. Rushmore the kids can find a place to play and the adults a place to relax and soak, all in natural mineral water.

INDEX

This index is designed to help you locate a listing when you start with the location name. The description of the location will be found on the page number given for that name.

Within the index the abbreviations listed below are used to identify the specific state or geographical area of the location.

The number shown after each state listed below is the page number where the KEY MAP of that state will be found.

AK=ALASKA / 22
CD=CANADA / 30
EA=EASTERN STATES / 176
ID=IDAHO / 86
MT=MONTANA / 150
OR=OREGON / 64
WA=WASHINGTON / 48
WY=WYOMING / 160

NUBP=NOT USABLE BY THE PUBLIC

WELLSPRING   WA 54
WEST PASS HOT SPRING   ID 102
WHISPERING OAKS   EA 191
WHITE LICKS HOT SPRINGS   ID 146
WHITEHORSE RANCH HOT SPRING
                         OR 65
WHITE SULPHER HOT SPRINGS   AK 28
WHITE TAIL PARK   EA 182
WHITE THORN LODGE   EA 179
WHITEY COX HOT SPRINGS   ID 92
WILD HORSE HOT SPRINGS   MT 159
WILD ROSE HOT SPRINGS   ID 109
WILLOW CREEK HOT SPRINGS   ID 112
WORSWICK HOT SPRINGS   ID 109

Z

ZIM'S HOT SPRINGS   ID 148

If you discover something at a hot springs
that needs to be revised, or happen to discover a new springs, jot the information
down here and send it to:
Aqua Thermal Access
55 Azalea Lane
Santa Cruz, CA 95060

Name			
Street			
City		State	Zip
		Order Quan.	Amount
Hot Springs and Hot Pools of the Northwest $16.95			
Hot Springs and Hot Pools of the Southwest $16.95			
Day Trips in Nature: California $14.95			
Postage: $3 first book, $2 each additional book			
Canadians: Please send in US dollars **BOOK** Make check to: AQUA THERMAL ACCESS (408) 426-2956 **MAIL ORDER** Mail to: 55 Azalea Lane, Santa Cruz, CA 95060			TOTAL

Name			
Street			
City		State	Zip
		Order Quan.	Amount
Hot Springs and Hot Pools of the Northwest $16.95			
Hot Springs and Hot Pools of the Southwest $16.95			
Day Trips in Nature: California $14.95			
Postage: $3 first book, $2 each additional book			
Canadians: Please send in US dollars **BOOK** Make check to: AQUA THERMAL ACCESS (408) 426-2956 **MAIL ORDER** Mail to: 55 Azalea Lane, Santa Cruz, CA 95060			TOTAL